Tending

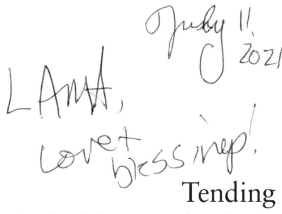

LANA,
love + blessing!

July 11,
2021

XO,
Amy

Tending

Parenthood and the Future of Work

Amy Henderson

NationBuilder Books, Los Angeles, CA
Copyright © 2021 by Amy Henderson
All rights reserved

Library of Congress Control Number 2021933652
nationbuilder.com

1 3 5 7 9 10 8 6 4 2

for my mom Beverly Scott

You have been invisible for far too long. I wrote this book to "see" you, honor you, and share your legacy. Thank you for giving me the foundation I needed to become this version of myself. You are loved and appreciated.

Foreword

"Do you have kids?"

In the U.S., this is a normal, everyday question. It's asked frequently in polite conversation to people seemingly over a certain age; a quick and easy way to break the ice.

But for all its normalcy, "do you have kids" is an extraordinarily intimate question. Beneath the socially acceptable yes or no replies, people might be trying and have yet to conceive a child, they might be pregnant but not sharing about it yet, they might have lost a child, they might not want children, they might have given a child up for adoption, or be in the process of adopting. They might be unable to have children, they might be becoming a parent, or already be a parent, a step-parent, a foster parent, a god parent, or any other kind of parent or guardian or caretaker. "Yes" is rarely just yes, and "no" is rarely just no.

People's relationship to becoming, being, or not being a parent is deeply personal, and has as many variations as there are human beings. Some of the greatest joys and the deepest sorrows available to us as people come in the form of our relationship to parenthood; it sits at the very core of who we are.

How then do we talk about parenthood in all its complexity, how do we wrestle with it, and create spaces for deeper conversations about it—especially in our workplaces?

For this incredibly personal experience is dramatically shaped by our environment: what kind of work we do; who our employer is; who our teammates are; and which state, province, or nation we live in. Is our employer understanding of the need to take parental leave? Are they able to subsidize it? Do they offer paternity leave? Does the government subsidize any portion? Is the workplace culture supportive of those with children?

I'll never forget meeting my Canadian husband's family for the first time. We were a few months into our relationship and I'd never been to Quebec before. One of his sisters had just had a baby and I asked her, naively, how much time she was allowed to take off for her maternity leave. I said something like, "Oh, I hope you're able to take at least three months." She looked at me like I was crazy and said, "No, I'll be off for the full year." I was baffled. She explained that the Canadian government supported a year of maternity leave. I was even more baffled. The people around us laughed at my American-ness. How strange I was to them.

It wasn't until later that I learned, as is detailed in this book, that the United States is the only country (alongside Papau New Guinea) with no federally paid maternity leave. Nor do we have, like many other countries do, some form of subsidized childcare for all citizens. Learning this was like waking up and realizing that all my pain-staking deliberations about how to both work and consider having a child existed inside a context I didn't even know I was in. What I thought was just a deeply personal struggle was revealed as a societal one, inextricably linked to what was considered "normal" in my country.

Then at the end of 2013, I met Amy Henderson. We were introduced through a friend and colleague who had asked me to help support Amy's work at #YesWe-Code. About a year into our professional relationship, NationBuilder began producing a documentary series about leadership in the internet age—created by the brilliant and multi-talented Laura Harris. Leaders were asked who they wanted to talk to for an in-depth, intimate conversation about the challenges they were facing. Laura asked who I wanted to talk to.

A few months later, Amy and I were filming our episode. What I remember about that conversation is that it went for three or four hours and felt like five minutes. It was raw and intense, neither of us holding back. I remember hearing Laura, helming one of the cameras, laughing as Amy described what it was like to "lose your brain" in your third trimester of pregnancy— which both Amy and Laura were in at that moment.

And I remember the way the conversation ended— with all of us in tears as Amy shared what she was experiencing being away from her two little ones while doing work she really cared about. She said, "they should be with me, especially when they're really little, they should be right here with me . . ."

When we screened the conversation for our staff a few months later, I remember the lights coming up and turning around in my seat to see a number of women—all mothers—sitting on the floor against the wall in the back of the auditorium crying. Amy's grief was a collective grief that illuminated the truth: something is desperately wrong with our collective reality when mothers, just a few weeks (sometimes days) after giving birth are made to choose between being with their newborn or earning an income that will put food on the table for their family. Or between being with their child or advancement in their career. I was witnessing that calculus firsthand, even in my own company.

So how do we solve this together?

We know that this issue does not just affect mothers or fathers or caregivers. It affects all of us. How we care for our caregivers, those tending the sick and young and vulnerable among us, says a lot about who we are as a society. How do I solve it, personally, as a leader of a company dedicated to the wellbeing of our employees? How do we afford it? I need help—we need help—not just to solve what's wrong, but to imagine what's possible.

That's where Amy's experience and this book come in. *Tending* is the result of years of painstaking research. Amy shares the synthesis of that research, but most importantly, she shares her story. It's intimate and raw and brave. She holds nothing back in her desire to help parents—and to help us all.

Tending is not just about parenthood. It is about our collective humanity. It illuminates not just the future of work—but the skills required to survive and thrive in the twenty-first century. It asks: who do we want to be together? And in her vulnerability and courage, alongside her academic rigor, Amy offers us an example of what could be—and who we could be to each other—as we create a world that puts tending at the center.

Lea Endres
April 2021

Introduction

I've spent the past twenty years looking at culture through the lens of parenthood. There is so much that is visible and available to us through this perspective. And it has shaped my life in unexpected ways.

Becoming a parent forced me to surrender my identity. Fortunately, I had already lost my sense of self once before, and I knew that I could put myself back together again. And because of this previous experience, I understood that the process of returning to myself required me to be both vulnerable and courageous. I had to be strong enough to look at the truth—both within me and around me—and not shy away from all that it revealed. And I had to take action. I had to roll up my sleeves and get into the muck of the messy experience of being alive today.

On March 11th, 2020, when the World Health Organization declared the Coronavirus a global pandemic, I had a visceral response as my body remembered the first time I'd lost my identity. My gut clenched tight; specifically, my duodenum, the valve responsible for releasing waste from my body, went into painful spasms. My breath became shallow. I couldn't sleep, and I spent long hours staring at the moon, which was a sliver shy of full, reliving in my mind's eye the last pandemic I'd encountered.

Two decades ago, I served as a Peace Corps volunteer in Malawi, East Africa during the AIDS pandemic. I lived alone in a rural village where UNAIDS estimated that one in six people were infected with the disease. That year, in addition to the AIDS pandemic, there was also a cholera outbreak and the national treatment center was 1000 yards from my cement house. On top of this, a drought left most Malawians with few viable crops and a severe shortage of food. Many people, particularly infants, died of starvation. After nearly a year in Malawi, I came home, as did many of the Peace Corps volunteers in my group, with Post Traumatic Stress Disorder.

After a long night of re-experiencing what I had felt in Malawi, I rose from my bed determined to call upon all I've learned in the past twenty years.

Soon after I returned home from the Peace Corps, I discovered that when I engaged in action—specifically, when I was working to push against the injustice and suffering in the world—it was easier to breathe, sleep at night, and look at myself in the mirror. So I threw myself into ventures designed to address the drastic inequity between my middle class, white background and the reality faced by under-resourced people all over the planet. A year after I returned home from Malawi, I was on the floor of the New York Stock Exchange completing six months of training to work with a firm that had a socially responsible portfolio. A few years later, when I learned that climate change was likely responsible for the drought I'd witnessed in Malawi, I cashed in everything I owned, including my car, and set off to the Arctic to learn more. After years of research and discovery, I eventually created a documentary short to capture some of the most courageous pioneers I encountered. The creation of this film led me to meet and work with Muhammad Yunus in Bangladesh, where I helped him expand his program training village women, mostly mothers, to become solar energy entrepreneurs using microcredit as a financial base for their services. In my early 30s, when I re-connected with and married my first date from junior high, I moved back to my childhood home in the Bay Area and started a program to empower young people from marginalized communities to start their own entrepreneurial projects—like the one run by young people in the food desert of West Oakland where they transport thousands of tons of fresh produce by bicycle to the corner liquor stores. In all of these experiences, I found that when communities are impacted by severe challenges, it is often the parents who suffer the most.

Then I became a mother. And many of the myths I'd once accepted as true—that gender inequity in the U.S. was mostly a thing of the past; that our success in life is based almost entirely on our individual efforts, independent of others—fell apart.

In 2015, after the birth of my third child, I went on a quest to learn more about the state of parenthood in America. From my time in under-resourced communities around the world, I was familiar with the suffering parents experience when they don't have even the bare minimum required for the survival of their children. Yet, I also knew—from first-hand experience and from conversations with other parents—that even the most resourced ones among us are facing challenges that all too often feel brutal or insurmountable. To highlight the extent of the struggle faced by parents in the U.S., I chose to focus on the experiences of people with professional success and all the privileges it affords. If parents who are middle class and above are being forced to make harsh sacrifices, then those among us with less financial security are facing especially dire circumstances. While the difficulties resourced parents face do not compare to the life-threatening circumstances encountered by mothers in countries like Malawi as well as in our own country, they are still real and valid. How parents are treated and held and protected and supported is the greatest reflection of a nation. It serves as a mirror into our culture. Because how we parent is the foundation of everything: what we value, what we stand for, who we are, and who we're becoming.

Five years ago, I started a business called TendLab to transform our culture's relationship to parenthood. In founding TendLab, I widely researched the question of how parenthood alters our hearts and minds. I conducted nearly 250 interviews with high-performing, financially-resourced parents, and looked into research from a broad range of disciplines, including neuroscience, evolutionary biology, management studies, game theory, and the future of work. I discovered that the U.S. is the least hospitable industrialized nation in the world for working moms and engaged working dads, and that there is a silent epidemic of shame and burnout among working moms, and increasingly among working dads. And yet, when a parent has the support they need, they are likely to develop skills that are not only valuable—but essential—for success in the modern workplace. Armed with this understanding, I am hired, through TendLab, to work with companies and their parents' groups—at places like Salesforce, Plum Organics, Accenture, FitBit, Lululemon, Yelp, Johnson & Johnson, Cloudflare, and Airbnb—to create the conditions necessary for parents to not only survive, but thrive.

When the COVID pandemic struck, the challenges already faced by working parents both increased and became visible. For people working remotely while sheltering-in-place with their kids, the gap between home life and work life became blurry, or even non-existent. And many companies, for the first time, began to recognize the needs of their parent employees.

My action in the face of COVID was to dig deeper in writing this book. In this narrative, I weave together the most challenging experiences of my life: recovering from PTSD in the wake of a pandemic and being a working mother and change agent on behalf of parents. While integrating these two experiences into the written word, I tapped into the raw and tender places within me. I also included the courageous stories of other parents and pioneers who have impacted me and my understanding. My intention in revealing these things is to both share with you, and remind myself, that our scars can become portals to deeper dimensions of healing. When we reckon with our pain, when we take the time to acknowledge and feel it, we increase our potency.

We cannot do this alone. To meet the transformation this moment offers we must recognize that our unique and specific heartaches exist inside the container of a bigger story, one in which we are all interconnected. Parenthood, possibly more than anything else, primes us to show up for the truth of this moment. But even if we never have children, we can care for others in need—elders, friends, relatives, and individuals in our greater community who may be in physical or emotional pain—and experience the transformation that tending to others can yield. May reading this book strengthen your capacity to play a part in building a better future for us all.

Chapter One

Giving birth to my first child, Clare, required a full-scale medical intervention at the hospital. Less than two years later, my second child, Aidan, was pulled from my body with the use of medical instruments at another hospital. Like so many things in motherhood, this was not what I had planned.

For most of my life, I was ambivalent about becoming a mother. When I did think about having kids, I imagined that it might be like acquiring a new handbag or two. I would just pick them up and carry them along with me while I went about changing the world. They would require some effort, I thought, some polishing, but they wouldn't impact my life all that much.

I had never even considered the possibility of being a stay-at-home mom. But my pregnancy with Clare, riddled as it was with health complications, forced me to reevaluate my priorities. My health practitioner had asked me, "Do you want your career or your kid? Because at the rate you're going, you can't have both." I answered this question by staying home for nearly two years.

Initially, I loved the experience. I discovered a world I'd never inhabited before, one that was slow, tender, profoundly intimate, and far outside the bounds of anything I'd been taught to even acknowledge, let alone value. When Clare was a newborn, we were rarely apart. Most mornings, I woke beside her as she'd been sleeping on my breast, and I gave her a bath. Doing this, I had the visceral memory that I, too, had been placed in warm water while my mom smiled down at my slippery, still amphibian-like body. Until then, I had forgotten how much my mom had been for me. That we'd been so intertwined. That she'd given me so much. And I hadn't realized how much it had mattered to me; how much it had informed my sense of myself in the world. Or that the memories still lived in me like reflexes, just waiting for the right stimulus to activate them. Clare brought all of them out. Her presence brought me into a lineage of women who'd been engaged in providing this type of care for generations—a line of mothers who had spent their days engaged in the physical and very real work of caring for their children.

One day when Clare was about six months old, she was sleeping beside me on a blanket while I sat on the grass in a meadow by a lake not far from our house. For at least thirty minutes, I watched the brittle fall leaves on the oak trees surrounding me amble towards the ground. And I remember marveling at my ability to be present with the moment. To just sit and watch my surroundings. And I knew that there was a power in this. But I didn't fully understand it at the time.

Even though I recognized and valued the work of caring for children, the initial novelty of the experience had worn off by the time my second child Aidan was born. Clare was twenty-one months old when I had

Aidan, and the prospect of tending to two children and their relentless needs, coupled with the lack of support or recognition for this work, depressed me.

Aidan was only a few days old when I left the kids with my husband Shane in order to walk around our neighborhood. Everything looked gray to me. I felt as though I was becoming transparent, beginning to disappear: When I looked down at my legs, they felt insignificant, as if they were less substantial than the ground beneath my feet. We couldn't afford for me to stay home any longer. And while the idea of separating from my kids, especially my newborn, felt like cutting out a chunk of the most raw part of my heart, I feared what would happen if I didn't return to the world I'd known before I became a mom. I needed to go back to work, and not just for financial reasons. It seemed that if I remained at home, I would eventually become so wispy and permeable that I might cease to exist.

Three months after Aidan was born, I began working with Van Jones, Cheryl Contee, and the musician Prince to co-found #YesWeCode, a national initiative to increase racial diversity in the tech sector. I was deeply invigorated by the work and felt myself gaining definition and color as the days, weeks, and months passed. I don't know if I came back to life because my work was visible to others and they could see me again or because I reconnected with the person I had been before I became a mom.

While at work, I tried to forget that I was a mom. At home, I tried to be the mom I'd been before I went back to work. I didn't know how to integrate the two experiences. I thought my career and my role as a mom were at odds with one another. That they were competing for my time and attention in a way that was negatively impacting both.

Back at work, I was delighted to discover that my time at home had changed me in beneficial ways. I experienced moments of great clarity, where my capacity to focus felt surreal. Before, I hadn't even been aware of any noise in my own mind. It was what I'd always known; and because I'd never experienced myself without it, I'd never questioned its existence. But when I returned to work, I realized that the unconscious din, which had run through my head like an out-of-tune radio station, came much less frequently. As a result, I was much more effective.

In a few years, neuroscientist Ruth Feldman, who teaches at the Yale School of Medicine, would explain to me how becoming a mother is likely to develop, among other things, an enhanced capacity to anchor feelings in the present moment, resonate with others' pain and emotions, simulate others' goals and actions in one's own brain, and collaborate well with others.

And I would also learn that neuroscientists Kelly Lambert and Craig Kinsley at the University of Richmond have found that female rats who have at least one litter are up to five times more efficient in catching prey and perform better on maze tests due to better memory recall. These changes lasted a lifetime and were true even for mice who didn't carry and birth the litter but who took responsibility for caring for the babies. Kinsley believes that the biological impulse to provide for one's babies rewires the brain to increase its efficiency. And as he told CNN in 2003, "The findings almost certainly apply to humans. People share most of their genes with rats, and such basic behaviors are very likely to be similar."

At the time, however, all I knew was that I had become a master of synthesis. Taking in what was around me and translating it into meaning. It was exhilarating. At times, it felt supernatural.

With #YesWeCode, Van had a clear view of what he wanted to create. One night, as we were driving home from a dinner party, he broke it down for me. I can't remember the exact phrases he strung together, but as I drove us in my Prius from the Oakland hills to his downtown hotel, I saw his vision. And, most importantly, I felt in my body a tingling sensation that coursed from my head down to my feet. I felt not just the possibility of the picture he painted, but the inevitability of it coming to fruition. My role was to find the opportunities that aligned with his vision—the people and places and ideas—and to link them up in effective action.

His vision was of several large stadiums located in major cities all over the United States full of Black and Brown kids working together on computers. Specifically, these kids would come together to code and to innovate new software, new applications, and new platforms that would address the problems they faced in their neighborhoods and create new pathways and paradigms for the enormous potential in their communities to be realized.

Almost nine months later we officially launched #YesWeCode in New Orleans, with Prince's support, at the Essence Music Festival.

On the opening night of the festival, as we drove in a Mercedes party bus to the Superdome to see Prince in concert, Van announced that our video, featuring one of our main partners—an Oakland hackathon of young men of color—was screening on every television in the massive amphitheater. In all the hallways on all the floors, the thousands of people filing into the concert were watching our video of young Black and Brown boys coding.

Even though I'd barely slept in a week, as we slipped through the New Orleans streets in our decadent bus with its blackened windows, I was radiantly awake with the promise of all that was to come. Besides Van and me, there were about fifty other people in our bus. They included our #YesWeCode team, high level executives we'd recruited from both Facebook and Google, and individuals from all over the country who'd launched the most effective nonprofits or foundations dedicated to educating kids of color about technology.

With our support, Kalimah Priforce's non-profit was running a hackathon for young people of color at the Essence Music Festival. That entire week, kids from all over the nation, including New Orleans' Lower 9th Ward, were sitting together over their laptops, receiving mentorship from some of the best technologists in the country, and designing apps to address the challenges in their communities, like the sex trafficking of minors, depression, foster kids' lack of access to fashionable clothes, and diabetes.

I'd spent much of that day, and the previous days, running around the festival arena monitoring the progress of the hackathon and the #YesWeCode technology village. Since that fateful conversation with Van nine months earlier, I'd been tracking down all of the groups working to teach youth technology skills. I'd traveled the country to meet with, learn from, and be inspired by all the great work these organizations were doing. The #YesWeCode technology village hosted many of the best of these organizations in rotating shifts, where the young folks and the adults who supported them shared their work with the hundreds of thousands of festival-goers who filtered through the arena. Trayvon Martin's mom, Sybrina Fulton, came to visit us at the #YesWeCode technology village. Her presence—heavy with the weight of her loss but strong in her commitment to catalyze change—galvanized all of us to recognize what was at stake in our work. Like Prince had asked Van and me on a prep call leading up to the festival, "Why is it that a Black kid in a hoodie, like Trayvon Martin, is associated with a thug, but a white kid is seen as a potential Mark Zuckerberg?"

On the way to Prince's concert, as our party bus pulled up to the stadium, I felt jubilant and giddy, like I was a bottle of champagne about to be uncorked. At the entrance to the Superdome, I saw a large group of kids wearing black shirts with the white #YesWe-Code logo emblazoned on them. As we stepped off the bus and headed through the VIP line to the backstage pre-party, Van leaned over and said to me, "Be ready . . . anything could happen! Prince might have us come up on stage. You just never know what he'll do . . ."

My husband would later say it was one of the best concerts of his life. Prince played many of his most well-loved songs—like "Purple Rain," and "Little Red Corvette"—and we were so close to the stage that I could practically touch it. At some point during the show, however, I started to pull away from the experience. By the time Prince did a quiet and thoughtful piano tribute to #YesWeCode, my breasts were engorged with milk and my eyes had grown bleary with exhaustion.

I'd pushed so hard to get to that point. For months, I'd been sleeping three to four hours a night. Committed to being present with my kids *and* determined to realize Van's vision, almost every night I'd put the kids to bed then stay up working on my computer until three or four in the morning. There were so many relationships to discover, develop, and deepen. I wanted to understand the landscape in which we were operating, so there was research to be done, too. And the impending date of our launch with Prince created an electric sense of urgency. I saw myself as the container for the energy we were building. The one who could hold it all together so that we could collectively create something bigger and better than any one of us could create on our own. All I had to do, as I saw it, was get us to the launch.

But after the concert, on the long walk back to our hotel, navigating through the post- concert traffic on unforgiving cobblestone streets that snagged the pointy heel of my shoes, I began to realize what was ahead of me.

I had been grateful to have tapped into a source of energy and momentum that lifted me out of the self-loathing I'd felt towards the end of my time as a stay-at-home mom. In co- founding #YesWeCode, I'd started to feel important again. My work was generating an income and giving me a reason to put on makeup and travel around the country to meet with passionate people improving their communities.

However, as I reached my hotel room at the end of the concert, the energy that had animated me for those many months dissipated.

When we arrived at our room, Aidan, who had been sleeping in a crib next to my mom in the adjacent room, woke up and cried out for me, his chubby arms reaching towards me with clenching fists. He hadn't seen much of me since we'd arrived in New Orleans, and he was hungry for me, not just for my milk but for my presence. That evening, he was particularly ravenous.

Lying beside Aidan that night, every time I began to slip into sleep, he would wake and scream out for me, desperate for the touch of my skin on his, the latch of his lips onto my breasts, and the drizzle of milk he could suckle. I grew increasingly anxious and frustrated as the night wore on and the sky slowly yielded from black to light blue. At dawn, a few birds began to call to each other outside the window of our room, and I fantasized about snapping their brittle necks. I could almost feel the cracking and popping sensation in my hands as I imagined twisting my fingers and severing the tendons and veins and bones that allowed them to sing with such obnoxious good cheer.

By the time we flew home from New Orleans five days later, I was operating at such a deficit, I could barely function. As I checked in for our flight at the airport, the humidity and my lack of sleep made my eyes feel like they were coated in oil. When I reached into my wallet in search of my driver's license, I couldn't distinguish it from my other cards. On the plane, Clare and Aidan fought over my attention, kicking each other and the seats all around us as they clamored for a spot on my lap or in my arms. During a layover that was probably only an hour or two long—but which felt much, much longer—while Shane went to change Aidan's diaper, Clare sat in the middle of the waiting area dumping her bag of pretzels out on the ground and grinding them into the grimy gray carpet with her hands before picking up the broken bits and shoving them in her mouth. I was conscious of the wide-eyed looks of my co-workers as I sat back and let her continue. I'd worked so hard to appear professional around my colleagues, many of whom I managed. Prior to our trip, they'd known me only as a woman with a carefully curated appearance. But as Clare's antics became more and more frantic—as she began jamming the pretzel shards into her already full mouth and the masticated, foamy bits fell out onto the floor— the crowd of strangers around us grew increasingly uncomfortable with her visible anxiety. All I could do was close my eyes and wish the moment away.

Chapter Two

Co-founding and leading a national organization is more than a full-time position. No matter how much I worked, there was always more to do. I tried to be a present parent with my kids, but they could never seem to get their fill of me. I didn't know how to care for myself when I was needed by so many. Even on the rare occasions when I got a full night's sleep, I still woke up feeling tired.

We'd been using protection and I was still breast-feeding Aidan, but I somehow got pregnant again when Aidan was barely one.

That winter, our entire family caught a nasty flu bug. For a week, my three-year-old, Clare, my not-yet-two-year-old, Aidan, Shane, and I, cycled through high fevers and vomiting. Every night during that week I was up holding the hot kids—or myself—over the toilet bowl. And I was beyond depleted.

Towards the end of the week, after Shane had recovered and returned to work, I was kneeling in my unwashed pajamas on our cracked linoleum floor wiping up chunks of flesh- colored vomit while Aidan, sobbing, clutched my ankles and Clare sat on the floor beside me yanking my greasy hair and demanding my attention, "Mommy . . . Mommy . . . Mommy!" Dark thoughts swirled in my head as I sponged the foul mess into a blue bucket. I imagined plugging my ears, opening my mouth, and screaming. I saw myself shaking my leg violently until Aidan fell off, then pinning Clare's hands to her sides so hard they turned white. I didn't trust myself not to hurt my children, so I just let them wail and yank and scream while I scrubbed.

My father-in-law, who was staying with us at the time, walked in the back door. He'd heard the crying and screaming from the driveway, and asked, "What's going on in here?" The kids, momentarily stunned by his presence, quieted. I looked up at him, my pregnant belly hanging low to the ground as I propped myself up on my hands and knees. He locked onto my bleak, red-rimmed eyes and said, "You know, Amy, the pioneer women in the Midwest, the ones who lived all alone out on the dusty prairies and never saw anyone but their husbands and their kids, and could never really get anything clean because the dust always covered everything as it howled in their ears . . . well, a lot of them just went crazy and killed their families and themselves."

As my father-in-law toddled out of the room and my kids resumed their yanking and screaming and crying, I felt I understood those mothers. And I finally acknowledged that my life had become unmanageable.

Up until that moment, I hadn't wanted to admit, even to myself, how much I was struggling. Even though I knew intellectually that other moms must also be having a hard time, I imagined that my situation was worse—either because of me and my unique shortcomings, or because of the bad decisions I'd made. And even after I had conceded to myself that I was incapable of handling everything, for some time, my shame prevented me from getting the help I knew I needed.

When I had Clare, I discovered my connection to an archetype which I call *The Mother*: a nurturing and viscerally powerful force that I now recognize can move into and through all of us, regardless of our gender or whether we have ever had kids. But after Aidan was born, because I didn't know how to live with this awareness, I ignored it.

Giving birth to my third child Grace brought it all back. I went into labor in the early evening and spent the first several hours in my home office, rocking and breathing on my ball chair. Relaxing and opening as the hours passed, I eagerly moved into the state I'd discovered while giving birth to my first two children. This time, I was hungry for the experience and what it offered: an opportunity to forge myself through the pain; and to give birth, not just to my daughter, but to a better version of myself.

In the early morning hours, I moved to the bathtub near our bedroom. Immersing myself in warm water was grounding and comforting as the contractions challenged me: Could I resist the instinct to tighten up with resistance? Could I relax my body, and even stretch open to meet the pain?

During my first labor, I had fought against the contractions. My mom had been there, and after one of the contractions had dissipated and my panting had slowed down, she'd picked up my slowly unfurling hand, held it in hers, looked into the huge pupils of my dilated eyes, and said, "Try softening when they come." It made no sense to me. How could I possibly relax when I was racked with pain? But slowly, I adopted her advice. Leaving one eye open. A few toes unclenched. Each time, my mom held my gaze, nodded encouragingly, smiled. It took effort to resist the instinct to round into a tight ball of self-protection. Incrementally, though, I learned to breathe rather than hold my breath when the contractions came. I started to trust the process rather than resist it. I learned to work with the contractions, to relax my tongue down from the roof of my mouth, and to stick it out, thick and loose, to let the heat building in me release with open-mouthed, slack-jawed, "Haaaaaas." "Yes, Amy," my mom had encouraged. "That's it." The pain didn't decrease, it morphed; as my body convulsed with waves that pulled me open from the inside out, I surrendered, breathing deeply into the sensations. I later learned that relaxing allowed a cocktail of beneficial hormones, particularly oxytocin, to course through my system.

While giving birth to Grace, I worked hard to welcome the contractions. And I succeeded. Maybe even too well.

When Shane ambled out of bed around four in the morning after hearing me grunting loudly, he opened the bathroom door to find me squatting by candlelight between the toilet and the tub. I looked up, squinting as he flicked on the fluorescent overhead lights, to announce, "She's coming."

Shane yawned, rubbed the stubble on his chin, and mumbled, "I'll go get the car."

"No time. She's coming now." "What?" His eyes opened wide. "No. I can drive really fast. Come on. Let's go."

"No time," I grunted.

Moments later, my mom was there. While I squatted with my elbows on the bathroom sink, anxiety blossomed like an ink stain in my chest. The glaring things—the bright, fluorescent, overhead lights and the absence of any medical professionals—threatened to eclipse the calm confidence I'd found when I was laboring by myself in the candle-lit bathtub. There were so many things, I now realized, that could go wrong.

My mom stood in the door, taking a picture with her phone of the matted hair stuck to my head and the blotchy red spots littering my naked, sweaty body. She cooed encouragement, "Great job. Everything's going perfectly. You've got this, Amy."

I closed my eyes and imagined myself connected to the wisdom of all of the mothers throughout time, and to *The Mother*, who was a part of all of us but so much greater than any one of us. And then, moments later, calmer and more at ease, I pushed, and Grace's head popped out. I felt her move between my legs.

"Stop touching her!" I yelled at Shane, whose hands, above a stack of folded white towels, were poised underneath me like a quarterback waiting for the snap.

"I'm not touching her!" Shane responded, his voice three octaves higher than normal.

"Amy," my mom calmly interjected, "she's moving all by herself. Everything's just fine, don't worry."

And then, with the next contraction, I pushed her all the way out. Shane caught her, but she was slippery and tumbled over onto the soft towels. Nearly hyperventilating, Shane picked her up and handed her to me.

She rooted around for my breast and when her mouth finally found my nipple and latched on, relief flooded through me. I grinned so hard my cheeks hurt. I'd just given birth. At home. With no nurses, or doctors, or midwives. And all appeared to be well.

The next day, while the end of the cut placenta cord was still attached to Grace's belly button, I resolved to reach out to the mom friends I admired—women who both embodied aspects of *The Mother* and who were also nailing it in their careers—to seek their counsel about how to do it all.

High on the euphoria of Grace's birth, delirious from a lack of sleep, and overwhelmed by the needs of my three kids all under the age of four, I would spit out a stream of words: "So . . . it's a lot. I feel a bit lost. And overwhelmed. And I have no idea how I'm going to make all of this work. But I also know something is happening to me. Something good. Something powerful. Important. What is it? Can you help me understand?"

The moms I called answered with big-hearted, generous responses. We wondered together: How was motherhood changing us? And how were we going to make it all work? Was it even possible? These first conversations proved so revelatory that I asked the mothers I admired to recommend other mothers that I should talk to.

Almost every single woman I spoke with said they'd been blindsided by how difficult it was to be a mom, and how they were regularly disappointed in themselves because they weren't showing up the way they thought they could be—or should be—in their careers, or with their kids, or both. But they had rarely, if ever, admitted this to anyone.

My cousin, a high-performer at Oracle with two sons, said, "It's brutal. And no one warns you."

Many moms remained silent because they feared speaking the truth would jeopardize their credibility.

"I feel like it's the greatest hoax out there," said one very successful mom, who'd spent much of her career in the C-Suite at Fortune 500 companies. "No one tells you how hard it's going to be to have kids and a career. No one admits how much they're struggling, because they're afraid it will make them look weak." She, like many other mothers I interviewed, took anti-anxiety and anti-depression medication to cope with it all. "It's the only way I can function," she admitted. "Otherwise, I'd just be in bed or broken down in tears all the time."

Discovering that almost every mom I spoke with regularly experienced shame and frequently felt over-whelmed both liberated and burdened me. It liberated me because it allowed me to see that I was not alone. I was not suffering because of my unique shortcomings or the bad choices I had made. I was struggling because being a mom today is really, really hard. Almost none of us—no matter how wealthy, or educated, or other-wise resourced we were—felt prepared enough to show up for the job the way we thought we should.

But if we were all suffering and no one was openly talking about it—*except to me*—then it meant I was responsible for doing something with this knowledge.

Especially because the second thing to surface in almost every conversation was the revelation that we were forging ourselves through motherhood. That motherhood was a chrysalis of sorts: it wrapped us up and made us feel as though we were lost in an exis-tence at odds with everything we'd ever been taught to value. But we cracked out of the cocoon of the experi-ence—again and again, in both big and small ways—to discover that we had evolved.

I was shocked to find that—before talking with me—the vast majority of the moms I interviewed had not even considered how motherhood might have had a positive impact on their lives, particularly on their ca-reers. Most of us are too inundated with negative messaging and bias, from the world around us and from within our own heads, to recognize this possibility. We haven't had the time, the space, or the support to reflect on and consider how our experience as a mom might be transforming us for the better.

As the mothers I interviewed continued to have similar "aha!" moments, I knew I had to continue talking to moms.

"What you're doing is very healing for us all," Elise Zelechowski the global head of the Office of Social Change Initiatives at Thoughtworks told me. "I've never thought about the things you've asked me today."

As the days, weeks, months, and years passed, and I continued to conduct interviews, I began to see each of these conversations as individual bricks—solid chunks that needed to be put to use. I took them all in, storing them in notes and reflecting on them during the quiet moments while I washed dishes or stood in the shower. I wasn't sure exactly what I was going to do with all that I was learning, but I trusted that it would become clear if I continued.

Chapter Three

Discovering a deep kinship with other mothers, particularly around the shame we all experienced, had a profound impact on me. Ever since coming home from the Peace Corps, I'd struggled to meaningfully connect with other people. At some level, I'd always felt like an outsider who didn't really belong. There were parts of me that no one else could see or understand. And to be honest, I had wanted some of these places within me to remain hidden.

At the end of my service in Malawi, on the longest leg of my journey home, I was upgraded to first class, where I struck up a conversation with the man seated next to me. A businessman from Malawi, he'd married an American woman and had three kids. Even though he frequently returned to visit his home country, he told me that he would never bring his kids to Malawi. "I want them to be true Americans," he explained. "And I want them to take everything for granted."

This conversation haunted me. He was right. Very few people I knew had ever been exposed to anything like what I'd seen in Malawi. They were blissfully unaware of how fragile life could be, and how easily it could be lost. But I knew. And I was ashamed of the person I'd been while I was living in a place where the thread between life and death was often as transparent and wispy as an abandoned spider web.

As a result, I've never been lonelier than when I came home from the Peace Corps. I was surrounded by people who loved me, but I couldn't receive their affection or give them mine. This improved, somewhat, over time. But I didn't feel as though I belonged anywhere until I became a mother. Having Clare placed me into a lineage of other mothers, both from my own ancestral lineage, and through all of human history, who had experienced the same life-altering transformation that comes from creating and being responsible for a life that is dependent on you for its survival. Connecting with my peers who were also grappling with the enormity of this responsibility—and who were willing to be honest with me about how often they thought they were failing, and how much shame they experienced as a result—allowed me to recognize that I was not alone.

As I continued to have conversations with moms, I also looked into other research. I wanted to understand the bigger picture. Why were we all struggling so much? And why couldn't we recognize motherhood's potential to positively transform us?

I found that it's harder to be a working mother in the United States than in any other country in the developed world. In sociologist Caitlyn Collins' book *Making Motherhood Work*, she contends that the work-family conflict faced by mothers in the U.S. is "a national crisis." This is rooted in three main things: our lack of federal policy to support parents; high (and increasing!) expectations of what it means to be a "good" mom; and the significant bias that women with children face in their careers.

Our lack of federal support for parents separates us from every other nation in the world. With the exception of Papau New Guinea, we are the only ones who have no federally paid maternity leave. This means that only 14% of employees in the U.S. have access to paid family leave. And, almost all of our economic counterparts in the developed world also provide at least some form of subsidized child care to all of their citizens, regardless of their income status. In the U.S., the absence of federal financial support for child care negatively affects the careers of three-quarters of parents with young children. And the United States is the only industrialized nation with no minimum standard for vacation and sick days.

Even though 70% of American mothers with children under the age of eighteen work outside the home—and most work full time—we expect moms to be present and invested in their kids' lives more than in previous generations. Working mothers today spend more time engaging with their children than stay-at-home moms did in the 1960s. This is especially true for highly educated mothers, as the amount of time we're spending in high-quality "interactive care," such as reading, storytelling, and playing, has almost tripled. To accomplish this, we're forsaking sleep, personal care, and leisure time.

And third, according to research conducted by professor Joan Williams at the UC Hastings Center for Work Life Balance, "mommy bias" is the greatest trigger for workplace discrimination. In 2007, Shelley Correll, then at Cornell University, found that mothers in the workforce are rated as significantly less competent, less intelligent, and less committed than women without children; and a mother is 79% less likely to be hired, and half as likely to get promoted, when compared to an equally qualified woman without a child. And it may be getting worse, as the number of women in the U.S. who are frightened to tell their boss they're pregnant has nearly doubled in the past five years from 12% to 21%. The United States has one of the largest gender pay gaps in the developed world, and motherhood is the biggest reason for this gap.

For all of these reasons, 43% of women end up staying home for two years when they become mothers. Just like me, most of these moms had never planned to pause their careers. We just couldn't figure out how to reconcile motherhood and work.

And it's even worse for mothers of color, who face the greatest challenges. First, they encounter greater discrimination in the workplace than white women. And second, the historical legacy and continued marginalization and exploitation of people of color means they often feel more compelled to make harsh choices.

One African American woman I interviewed, a high level executive at a Fortune 250 company, explained how her grandfather had been born to parents who were slaves, and how her own father had been forced to sleep in ditches and open fields when he migrated from the South to the West Coast because he couldn't find any lodging that would accommodate Black people. Her father had made the perilous journey to build a better life for his children, and she felt the heavy responsibility of honoring all that he'd done to give her the opportunities he'd never been afforded. When she became a mom, it was not an option for her to "indulge" in deepening her early bond with her newborn. When her child was not yet one, her employer assigned her to an intensive three-month project in another state and she felt as though she had no choice but to accept the assignment and leave her baby at home with her husband and a caretaker.

After the birth of her second child, another mother of color felt compelled to go back to work even before her short six-week leave was over. When she'd taken the full six weeks of leave with her first child it had been too painful to bond and then return to the long hours of work her career mandated. She didn't want to go through the same emotionally "brutal" separation again, and she felt that her early return would help to mitigate the bias that she—a Black woman and a mother—inevitably encountered. "I was still leaking all over," she said to me, "I hadn't yet fully healed from giving birth, and I kept having to sneak into the bathroom to change my clothes and pull myself together. I couldn't afford to let anyone know what I was going through."

As I continued to hear similar stories from mothers of color, I was struck by the way they felt compelled to make sacrifices—more than most white mothers—in their relationships with their children. For many women, these sacrifices intensified the feelings of isolation and loneliness that they—as women of color—were already experiencing at work.

All of this research, and my on-going interviews with moms, helped me to place myself inside the container of a bigger story. I eventually realized that I not only belonged inside this story, I also had a role to play in developing it.

Chapter Four

Half-way through my maternity leave with Grace, Shane and I decided to take our motorhome to Montana to stay at his dad's ranch. As we were packing, my mom handed me a two-inch plastic Buzz Lightyear doll. "This is Aidan's favorite toy," she told me. I had never seen it. I had no memory of Aidan ever playing with it. But I shoved the toy in my bag as we rushed to get out the door.

Five minutes down the road, Aidan started shouting, "Buzz! Buzz!" And when I handed him the plastic toy, he cradled it to his chest with a smile.

I began to wonder what else I wasn't seeing.

Almost every weekday for the past year, I'd dropped Clare and Aidan off at the same daycare. Every morning, Aidan had sobbed and clung to me, his pudgy fists clutching and twisting my clothes until his knuckles turned white. And while Clare wasn't as outwardly upset, I could sense her distress in her downturned, red face, and the way her feet slowed and stumbled as we moved from the car to the door of the center.

Every time I wrenched Aidan's hands out of my wrinkled shirt to hand him over to the woman running the center, I ignored the stabbing pain in my chest. And as I turned my back on him and stoic Clare, I told myself the daycare center was a good enough place for them to be.

The center had been recommended by a mom I held in high regard. A highly educated woman, she'd put her career on pause to stay home with her children. To socialize her toddler, she sent her to the center for two afternoons a week.

Our kids, however, were there much longer, averaging more than fifty hours at the center in any given week.

Our other friends who also had a child in the center full-time, pulled their son out when, after weeks of sobbing at drop-off time, he had eventually refused to get out of the car. He was an unusual child, I told myself, who had special needs.

Aidan's distress at getting dropped off at the center didn't diminish with time, as other working moms had assured me it would. It seemed to get worse. In response, my mom had stepped in to watch Aidan on Fridays.

Later, I learned from one of the part-time caretakers at the center that crying children were often put in a large, dark room by themselves until they quieted, which could take over an hour.

While in Montana, as I watched how inconsolable Aidan was if I stepped out of his sight, the certainty that the center was not a "good enough place" for my kids crashed into my awareness.

How had I ignored or denied it for so long?

The conversations I continued to have with other mothers gave me the courage and the space I needed to answer this question.

I thought taking my kids to daycare was abandoning them. And the heavy, gray cloud of this feeling wrapped its dense tendrils around my chest and made it hard for me to breathe. So I held my breath, ignored it, and charged forward. Anything that delayed my departure—wiping a snotty nose or tending to an untied shoe—made me feel like a caged animal struggling to escape, and I lashed out at my kids with a ferocity that made me cringe.

Because I felt like I was abandoning them, I was certain that we would all ache every time I walked away, no matter where I left them. However, in order to function, I denied my feelings and grew to resent my kids for having their own. And because I was focused on just getting through it, I hadn't been willing to see the more nuanced truth of their experience. Yes, they were aching because they did want me, but they were also suffering because the center was a harsh place.

On a dark night when Grace couldn't sleep, I lay awake staring out the window at the abundance of stars visible in the rural Montana sky. I asked myself if I'd kept them at a daycare that was not warm and nurturing because I was afraid of being replaced. Did I fear them abandoning me for another and loving someone else more than me because I had abandoned them to go back to work?

Bringing the light of my awareness into the shadowy places within my mind and heart was not easy. But it was necessary. Before I could make better decisions, I had to look at all of the reasons I'd made—and stuck with—a poor one. And once I'd been honest with myself about all my many possible motivations, I felt less burdened by my shame or my fears. This created the space for me to be curious: What was best for the kids? And for me? Who else has asked these questions? And what had they discovered?

Evolutionary anthropologist Sarah Hrdy is widely considered "[t]he leading scientific authority on motherhood" (Biologist E.O. Wilson). When she had her first child in 1977, she was a postdoc at Harvard. Even though she worked hard to maintain a close connection with her daughter, she was harshly judged for not sacrificing her career to focus exclusively on her child.

Sarah's main mentor at the time, Harvard biologist Robert Trivers, one of the nation's preeminent evolutionary theorists, told a journalist who was writing an article about her, "Sarah ought to devote more time and study and thought to raising a healthy daughter. That way misery won't keep travelling down the generations."

This painful comment struck a deep chord in Sarah. She did not blame Trivers for bluntly stating what so many Harvard professors, virtually all male in those days, believed. The comment hit her so hard because, as she said in a later interview, "I feared that Bob Trivers might be right!"

This difficult and conflicted period in Sarah's life eventually led to her most significant scientific breakthroughs. "Fortunately," she told me, "I was never content to agonize when I could analyze instead." Ultimately, Sarah's work proved revolutionary in explaining the history of human evolution and the origins of human intelligence.

Thanks to Sarah's decades of research, I now understand several critical things.

First, a woman's ability to develop and maintain her "maternal instinct" is highly dependent on the level of support she receives. If she does not have other people in her life who help her tend to her child, she may not unlock her own ability to bond with and care for her child.

Second, career ambition and motherhood are not opposed to one another. Rather, "they are inseparably linked and natural. Striving for clout," Hrdy states, "is genetically programmed into our psyches." Female ambition is not pathological. Seeking status in our social hierarchies is as critical to females as it is to males, if not more so. Over tens of millions of years, the survival rate of monkey and ape infants correlated with the social clout of their mothers. Over time, "Mother Nature," Hrdy's personal metaphor for Darwinian natural selection, favored mothers who maintained advantageous social connections. From an evolutionary standpoint, we mothers aren't meant to raise our kids in isolation all on our own. Stay-at-home mothers are rare in the history of humans and our closest related primate ancestors. "Mothers have worked for as long as our species has existed, and they have depended on others to help them rear their children," Hrdy found.

Third, infants cared for by both their mothers and others were most likely to survive and prosper. In order to feel secure, children need an enormous amount of physical affection and responsive attention. From an evolutionary standpoint, the infants who received the care and affection of others—who developed their own capacity to care about others, as well as how they were perceived by others—were most likely to survive. And over time, this led to the emergence of prosocial behaviors such as empathy, altruism, and the ability to collaborate with others.

And fourth, our sophisticated and developmentally advanced society is rooted in our ancient history of communal care. Roughly 2.6 million years ago, when our great ancestors became communal in the care of our young, they altered the trajectory of our brains' development.

Have you ever wondered why humans are the most dominant species on the planet? As Victoria Dimitra-kopoulos of Project BrainHeart, explained it to me, "Relative to the size of our bodies, we do not have the largest brains, whales do; we do not have the most neurons, elephants do; and we are not even the ones with the most neocortical neurons, the dolphins are. So why are humans at the top of the food chain? The so-called 'human advantage' has not yet been found in any individual brain. What is special about human brains is how they entice us to connect with other brains to form a collective brain which we access both for regulation and knowledge."

Relative to other primates, humans have the greatest capacity for trust and curiosity: our brains are relentless about figuring out and possibly accepting what others may know that we might not. This innate curiosity gives us a stronger ability to suspend our urges for aggression, suspend our agenda long enough to wonder what is on other people's minds, and suspend disbelief. Humans are more likely than any other primate to follow others if we believe they have something valuable to teach us. Scientists call this core set of skills prosocial behavior, which leads to shared intentionality. And this neurological capacity to collaborate effectively is what led to the creation of language, complex technologies, and art, as well as formalized norms and institutions.

Evolutionarily, we've been optimizing our ability to collaborate ever since we became communal in the care of our young. And while humans evolved over millions of years to develop this propensity, any one individual's ability to access their capacity to collaborate is enhanced by the presence of multiple nurturing caregivers in their own childhood.

After discovering Sarah Hrdy's research, I felt empowered to make decisions that were better for my kids and for me. To care for Grace and Aidan, we had a wonderfully warm and nurturing au pair from Brazil named Dayane come live in our home. It was still hard for me to break away from them in the morning, as Grace and Aidan would both cry, but I understood that Dayane's presence in our lives was ultimately good. For all of us.

For Clare, we miraculously secured a spot at a preschool that normally had a several-years-long wait list. We were very lucky, as child care in our area is severely limited.

Located on a small farm in an urban neighborhood, Clare's new preschool was an anomaly. It had been run by the same family for several decades and most of the teacher's had worked there for more than twenty years. Because the United States has no federal subsidies for child care, most child care workers earn the same amount as gas station attendants. As a result, child care facilities usually have extremely high turnover rates because employees can't earn a living wage.

On the morning of my first day back to work from maternity leave, I brought four-year- old Clare to her first day at her new preschool. Her hands shook as she placed her pink My Little Pony lunchbox on the hook beside her name. And later, as I felt my own legs shaking in the elevator on my way to my office, I thought of her courage as she'd turned around to smile at her new classmates. I put on a brave face as I went out to greet the colleagues I hadn't seen in twelve weeks. Even though Clare and I were not physically together, the similarity of our experiences made me feel deeply connected to her. And, when I picked her up at the end of the day, her expression seemed to mirror my own expression of exhilarated and overwhelmed exhaustion. Our hug of greeting was one of shared understanding.

The next day at drop off, I noticed Clare's legs moving faster, rather than stumbling and slowing down, as she neared the entrance to her classroom. And soon after, she announced that she loved her school, something she had never done when she'd been going to the other daycare center.

On the days when I worked from home, I could see the gentle affection between Dayane, Grace, and Aidan. While I did have twinges of jealousy—and some part of me worried that they would grow to love Dayane more than me—when I was honest with myself about these feelings, they lost their hold on me. And I could focus on how Dayane's loving way of engaging with my kids was good for all of us.

Chapter Five

I was opposed to the idea when some of my friends suggested that I also interview dads. I didn't think men could ever understand or experience the highs or the lows of motherhood. And many of the moms I interviewed felt the same way.

Many of us resented our husbands. They just didn't get it, we lamented to each other. They didn't feel responsible for the messes—the physical ones, or the emotional ones.

But many of us also believed, at either a conscious or an unconscious level, that we were supposed to do the majority of the work—especially when it came to caring for our kids—because we were better suited for the job. I hadn't expected to feel this way. Like many other women I knew, I had chosen my husband because I wanted a partnership with someone who would support my career goals, and I had assumed that he would be a hands-on father. Before we married and had kids, we had agreed that he would be the caretaker so that I could pursue my career. However, once I became a mom, it was much harder for me to see how he could match my ability to care for our children.

I'd carried our children in my womb, birthed them, and nursed them. In the role of nurturer, I suddenly felt biologically superior to my husband.

One day while I sat on the bathroom floor covered in Aidan's diarrhea, Shane stood in the doorway with his feet firmly planted on the carpet in the hallway and narrated the scene like a sport's commentator, "Whoa, son! You are your daddy's boy. That smells so foul! And it's all the way up your back to the base of your neck. It's even in your hair!"

Working hard to be upbeat and good-natured as I stripped off Aidan's clothes and ran the bathwater, I told Shane, "I don't want you to feel left out. This is all good stuff . . . You can step in here anytime"

"Thanks for the offer," Shane said, laughing. "But I'll pass!"

"Can you just take this bucket of soiled clothes and towels into the laundry room for me?" I asked. "I don't want to smell it in here."

Aidan had just had an explosive bout of diarrhea in the living room and, even though Shane and I had both been in the room when it happened, I'd been the one who'd swooped in to pick Aidan up and carry him into the bathroom.

The next day, when I found the bucket sitting untouched in the laundry room, I was no longer good-natured.

"Why am I the only one who has to deal with all the shit around here?" I yelled at Shane. "I thought when I asked you to bring it to the laundry room that you would clean it out."

"You only asked me to carry it into the laundry room," Shane said in a reasonable defense.

"Yes, but I assumed you would clean it without me having to walk you through each step."

So began one of the many conversations my husband and I have had about who is responsible for the shit in our house.

I never thought it would be like this.

When I was in college, my grandparents surprised me one weekend by visiting me at the apartment I shared with three other girls. Back then, I had made the conscious decision not to scrub the grimy toilet bowl in our shared bathroom. I was conflicted about the choice, but I had made it. I wanted my grandparents to see that we were liberated women. We were honor students who spent our time in chemistry labs and libraries. Having a clean toilet was not a priority for us. And I suppose some part of me wanted to show both of them that I hadn't been trapped in the small world that was my grandmother's domain.

I'll never forget my grandmother's face when she walked out of the bathroom. She was a tall, strong woman with a loud voice and warm, sky-blue eyes. When she stepped out of the bathroom, she had a disoriented look on her face and her eyes were glossed over. My attempt to prove how modern and successful I was had shamed her, and she was trying to recover.

I wish I could go back to that moment and tell her what I know now.

When I became a mom, my grandmother's world opened up to me. Among other things, I started to really care—obsess even—about the cleanliness of everything in our house. Especially our toilets. I was partly preoccupied with what other people would think. While I'd been proud of my poor housekeeping before I had kids, after becoming a mom, I didn't want anyone to judge me for having a dirty house. I hadn't fully registered how our society had taught me that a clean house is a fundamental part of being a "good" mom. But it was also because germs lead to illness, and when our kids got sick, I had to drop everything I had planned to take care of them. Having a dirty house meant we were more susceptible to sickness, and one sick kid was likely to lead to three sick kids. And a sick husband. And what if I got sick too?

My husband rarely seemed to notice the filth. And it drove me crazy that he didn't share the same level of responsibility or investment in the cleanliness of our house and kids as I did.

Thankfully, as I interviewed mothers who had experienced meteoric success in their careers, I was forced to reconsider how I viewed my husband's capacity to show up at home.

One of the women I interviewed was Shellye Archambeau, who at the time of our interview was the CEO of MetricStream, a Silicon Valley tech company with over 1,000 employees. The daughter of a stay-at-home mom and a dad without a college degree, Shellye was number two in *Business Insider*'s 2013 list of "The 25 Most Influential African-Americans In Technology."

Shellye told me that her husband deserved much of the credit for her success because he carried the bulk of the responsibility for caring for their home and children. Several studies have shown that when men show up for fatherhood, especially during the early childhood years, it has a profoundly positive impact on their wives' careers.

"At first," Shellye told me, "there were times when I tried to micromanage the way my husband did things at home, and he had to stop me and say, 'Look, I'm going to do it the way I want to do it.' And initially that was hard for me, because his way was not my way."

In one of her class pictures, Shellye's daughter was wearing two braids that were supposed to be pinned up on her head, but one had fallen down. "While my husband was doing her hair, I could've stepped in and done it better," Shellye said, "but that would've disempowered him."

After I interviewed Shellye, I asked my husband if I blocked him from stepping in at home. Looking at me sideways, he said, "You never even let me hold our first kid until she was six months old."

Exasperated, I told him, "I would've been happy to let you hold her, especially when she woke up every two hours at night. But you never got up to get her."

"I never heard her cry," he said.

This was true. He had happily snored through Clare's crying, while I, a previously sound sleeper, sat bolt upright in bed the second she began to whimper.

"You could've gotten me up," my husband told me. "I would've been happy to go and get her. Or Aidan. Or even Grace, now."

After that conversation, I started shaking my snoring husband awake when Grace cried at night. True to his word, he got up to hold her and soothe her back to sleep. And we discovered that when he went to her at night, she settled down faster and stayed asleep longer.

A few months after Shane started tending to Grace at night, we were having breakfast in the kitchen when he mentioned that he'd gotten up with her the night before.

"What?" I said. "You heard her cry and I didn't."

"Yep," he said with a wink. So, I began to interview dads, too.

The neuroscientist I mentioned in Chapter One, Ruth Feldman, has spent the past twenty years studying the impact of parenting on the brain. She told me, "The adult human brain is capable of the greatest plasticity during the year surrounding the birth of one's child, and that's true for both moms and dads."

During the lifespan of a human being, according to Feldman, the greatest potential for plasticity is in the first six years of a child's life, and in the first year of parenting for adults. I knew that my kids' brains were rapidly developing. It was visible—they learned to sit up, crawl, eat, walk, and talk. And I sensed that I was also experiencing drastic neurological changes. But I struggled to see how this was equally available to my husband.

"While only mothers experience pregnancy, birth, and lactation," Feldman explained to me, "evolution created other pathways for the adaptation to the parental role in human fathers, and these alternative pathways come with practice, attunement, and day-by-day caregiving."

Women who give birth to their babies are flooded with a range of hormones, particularly oxytocin, which primes their neurological systems to develop the capacity to respond to the needs of their infants, what Feldman calls "the maternal pathways." The brains of birth mothers are therefore ready to learn how to effectively care for their babies. Feldman's research indicates that dads, even non-biological fathers, may have their brains altered in response to parenthood as much as moms, but that this process happens through a different neural system, or "paternal pathway." Unlike the maternal pathway, which is automatically primed through gestation, birth, and breast feeding, the paternal pathway must be primed more intentionally. That is, a dad has to engage in activities which will stimulate these distinct structures in his brain. "It's not just fathers who think about or play with their kids," Feldman explained to me. "In order for this brain plasticity to occur, a father needs to give their baby baths, feed them, and get up with them when they cry at night." He needs to assume a caregiving role and take it up with diligence, commitment, and perseverance. A dad's ability to sensitize his neurobiological system is dependent on him being responsible for many of the daily tasks necessary to care for his child during the first year of their life.

This, scientists theorize, is because evolutionary adaptations occur when survival is at stake. Up until 150 years ago, roughly every third woman died in childbirth. In order for babies to survive, all adults, including men, needed to have the latent ability to develop the skills necessary to care for their children.

Feldman found that, in general, when dads first show up for caretaking, they have to "think" through everything. This is because fatherhood is likely to initially activate a region of the brain associated with mentalizing behavior. They have to "think" through all the reasons why their baby might be crying: Are they hungry? Thirsty? Tired? Do they need their diaper changed?

Adam Rhuberg, the Director of Analytics at Upwork, has twice taken twelve weeks of parental leave to stay home alone with his newborns after his wife went back to work. When I interviewed him, he described the activation of his mentalizing network. "If you're alone, you have to figure out how to empathize with a three or four month-old, and you have to learn to pick up the non-verbal clues, like the wrinkle in the forehead or the pulling on the ear, and how this means they're sleepy and they need a nap. If you miss these signs, you have to live with the consequences."

According to Feldman's research, and that of others, the amygdala is one of the critical structures associated with the maternal pathway. Our amygdala is an essential part of our subconscious brain that we share with all other mammals. It facilitates our emotional memories, our feelings and expression of emotions, and our ability to recognize the emotions of others. As Feldman explained to me, when researchers forced mice to interact using only their emotional brain by disconnecting the amygdala from the regions of the brain associated with "thinking," mother mice were still good moms. When the amygdala is fully activated and functioning, moms may not even need to think to parent; instinct suffices. This even appears to be true for female mice who don't give birth to the litter, but who take primary responsibility for caring for them.

Initially, the paternal pathway does not activate the amygdala and its associated structures. However, Feldman has found that a father's degree of engagement with his child appears to be correlated with his ability to turn on this region of his brain. Beyond just the mentalizing network developed in secondary caretaking fathers, according to Feldman, "in primary caregiving dads you can have the full parental network system activated to its highest volume." In other words, engaged dads, even non-biological fathers, can develop their ability to reflexively and intuitively respond to the needs of their infants.

Recently, Feldman published a review of all of the research conducted on the impact of parenting on the brain. In the article, she says that parents who develop the full parental network system to its highest volume are likely to develop many skills, including: an enhanced capacity to anchor their feelings in the present moment, resonate with others' pain and emotion, simulate others' goals and actions in their own brain, and collaborate well with others.

As I interviewed fathers who were deeply involved in caring for their children, I was amazed by the depth of the transformation they experienced, especially when they served as primary caretakers.

One of the dads whose story forced me to reconsider my position on fatherhood, Matt Markovich spent seven years at home with his two children. And while he did some consulting work during this time, his wife worked full-time outside the home and was their primary breadwinner.

Matt treasures the time he spent with his kids. As he said, "I wouldn't trade anything for the insights I gained about my kids, the total picture of being a caregiver, and, as crazy as it may sound, my own humanity. It was a truly existential journey. It challenged and changed me on every level, but it was also very difficult. When you don't speak to another adult for eight hours at a time and your kids are largely non-verbal, you have a lot of time in your own head," he told me. "Especially when they're small, when they're not interactive. When you're not out doing things. I was much better equipped to enjoy the babyhood of our second child, but the first came with a very steep learning curve."

At a dinner party one night, a friend of Matt's, whom he described as "a high-powered venture guy who travels around the world," was talking disparagingly about his wife. She was staying home with their newborn and she described the experience as super-stressful and enough to make her feel crazy. Matt's friend thought his wife was being melodramatic. Matt stepped in to explain, "No, man, this may seem extreme to you, but you must understand, being at home alone has a lot in common with being in solitary confinement. When you are responsible for keeping another human being alive who has no ability to interact with you besides crying and smiling, it's really difficult. You feel like you're walking around with a grenade with the pin pulled. If you let it go, it's going to blow up. You can read all the books you want, but there's still never getting over the sense that 'You have to keep this being alive.' Not that it's always that level of sustained anxiety, but you're always on."

Similar to the way I had felt transparent when I was a stay-at-home mom, Matt said, "When you're responsible for a newborn, if you don't make a point to get out of the house to interact with people, you begin to

lose a sense of individual identity. We are social crea-
tures and, over time, that kind of withdrawal and lack
of regular interaction begins to erode your sense of self.
Unless you make a point of being active and engaged
with other adults, staying at home with a baby is a really weird, isolating, surreal experience."

It isn't just Matt who understands how hard it is
to stay home with a child. Every primary caretaking
father I interviewed described the experience as extremely stressful. As Griffin Caprio, the Founder of
Chicago-based podcasting company Dante32, who was
home alone for eight hours a day for the first sixteen
months of his son's life, says, "It was 100% dependent
on me to not let him get killed."

Beyond just the stress of keeping a child alive, I
found that stay-at-home dads were plagued by the
same doubts that I—and most of the former stay-at-
home moms I spoke with—had also faced.

Matt Markovich said he'd thought of himself as
fairly confident and self-assured. But after being home
with his sons for such a long stretch of time, he found
himself worrying if he was even capable of returning to
full-time work. Could he still perform? Had he become
irrelevant? And even beyond that, what was his worth
in the world?

Ray Stompton and his partner had been equal in
their careers—both attorneys with their own successful practices—when Ray chose to stop working so he
could serve as the caretaker for their soon-to-be adopt-

ed child. Almost immediately, Ray's social standing diminished among their family and their circle of friends. And Ray's status in his marriage with his husband also began to suffer as Ray internalized the belief that his role as a stay-at-home parent made him less important. "My job as a stay-at-home parent is the hardest job I've ever had, but no one seems to recognize or value the work I now do," he told me, "Even though I know what I'm doing matters, that it's critically important, sometimes I struggle—even in my own head—to know my worth."

And just like moms, primary caretaking dads often feel as though returning to work is sacrificing their relationships with their kids. Griffin Caprio felt like he was abandoning his son when he dropped him off at daycare for the first time. He said he still feels guilty about it, even though his son is now in elementary school.

And dads can instinctively respond to diarrhea.

Ben Wang, the Co-Founder and CEO of Chimera Bioengineering, served as the primary caretaker for his infant twin daughters while his wife battled an aggressive form of leukemia. When one of his twins was about one year old, he was changing her diaper when he noticed that she was about to poop. Without thinking, he reflexively reached out to intercept the stream of what became a "geyser of liquid diarrhea."

As he relayed it to me, "I stuck my hand out to intercept the poop stream and felt an incredible sense of relief that I was able to prevent it from splattering everywhere. And as I felt the still warm liquid dripping off of my hand, I noticed my usually ever-present gag reflex didn't kick in. Instead, I grabbed a few wipes, a couple for my daughter and a couple dozen for me, and slapped a clean diaper on her. The feeling of being mildly impressed at my own coordination was brief. I knew I was already a diaper pro having had changed about 80% of all their diapers, not for any particular penchant, but rather to protect my wife, who was susceptible to infections while recovering from multiple rounds of chemotherapy and bone marrow transplants. I wanted to spare her the remote possibility that changing diapers would land her in the ER. My karate chop, reflexive block of my daughter's diarrhea was both a functional way of protecting my wife's health and a metaphor for how close my relationship with my daughters had become."

Ben's wife passed away when his twin girls were two-and-half years-old. As Ben shares, "There are no real silver linings to my wife being gone, but I recognize that if she were never sick, I might have gone on to live a defaulted life, emphasizing work over volunteering at their school and ultimately spending less time with my daughters. Our lives aren't perfect; they stay at after-school care while I work, and I am grateful my nanny watches them frequently when I have to work late or travel. Recently, they told me that they miss their mom, perhaps truly missing her or missing out on a key relationship. But I am relieved for how happy and well-adjusted they are, how much our community steps up to pick them up when they fall and to celebrate their victories. Most of all I am grateful that through the time I've spent with them, I have incredibly strong, multifaceted relationships with these amazing human beings."

Unfortunately, most men today do significantly less child care than their spouses, especially during the early years. And even when it's available to them, they don't take any significant parental leave because they are worried it will jeopardize their careers.

However, men have historically experienced a sizable uptick in their careers when they have kids, often because fatherhood makes them seem more "stable" and "committed." Michelle Budig, a sociologist from the University of Michigan who has studied this phenomenon, calls it the "Fatherhood Bonus": on average, fathers earn $5,000 more per year than men of the same age and experience without children. That said, this may only be true if a dad doesn't appear to have any significant caregiving responsibilities. If they do, they are likely to be stigmatized and passed over for promotions, raises, and high-profile assignments.

Much of this stigma comes from assumptions about what parental leave, and child care in general, means for work performance. If you're a man who takes leave or carries some of the responsibility for caring for your children, the thinking goes, you mustn't be serious about your job.

Fortunately, change is coming. A study conducted by Ernst and Young in 2013 found that millennials—of both sexes—expect to engage meaningfully with their children without sacrificing their career ambition.

Mary Beth Ferrante of WRK/360, an organization working to support parents inside companies, says that 30 – 40% of the parents who sign up for their Core Working Parents program are dads. Mary Beth has found that, "dads today are struggling with wanting to do more at home than previous generations but are uncertain how to navigate this new commitment to their families in a workplace that is still stuck in the past."

The advocacy organization PL+US, which is advocating for legislation guaranteeing paid family leave for everyone in the United States, recently conducted a poll about fatherhood in America and they found that 84% of expecting fathers plan to take leave, but only half believe their employer supports them. Nearly a third of dads think that taking leave could negatively impact their careers; fathers at all income levels are more likely to be interested in working for a company that offers paid leave; two out of three fathers surveyed said paid leave benefits would increase their interest in working for a company; and finally, 82% of dads surveyed want to equally share the responsibility of parenting.

And dads are beginning to successfully advocate for themselves.

Derek Rotondo filed a class action lawsuit against his employer, JP Morgan Chase, claiming that male employees were being discriminated against because they didn't receive the same amount of paid parental leave as women. In 2019, JP Morgan Chase paid a settlement of $5 million dollars and made alterations to their parental leave policy.

The American Civil Liberties Union, which represented Rotondo in the case, said this marks the first settlement of its kind and may serve as a harbinger of things to come, as there is growing pressure on employers to adopt gender-neutral paid-leave policies that encourage more equitable caregiving roles in the home. Recent data bears this out. The settlement encouraged other employers to move away from leave policies that designate a "primary" and a "secondary" caregiver and towards gender-neutral leave policies.

After winning his lawsuit, Derek Rotondo stayed home for several weeks when his second child, Lincoln, was born. The experience allowed him to discover the transformation that parenthood offers. "I think all new dads . . . kind of assume that babies are these mysterious, magical beings and that only the mothers can speak the language," Rotondo told *The Washington Post*. "But I found that that's not really true."

Now, just like with Shane and Grace, when Rotondo's son wakes up in the middle of the night, he is the go-to parent who calms him down so he can fall back asleep.

Sharing the responsibility of caring for our kids has long-term implications.

Recent research out of Feldman's lab shows that the way we co-parent impacts the development of our brains. Specifically, she's found that the quality of our co-parental bond has a significant impact on us. Parents who engage in a collaborative co-parenting relationship in which they constructively work together to care for their child or children, are likely to activate the regions of the brain associated with flexible, goal-directed behavior: altruism; empathy, and an enhanced capacity to collaborate. In contrast, parents who develop undermining co-parenting relationships in which they are combative and at odds with each other, are likely to activate the regions of the brain associated with fear and anxiety.

Unfortunately, many of the moms and dads I interviewed said they are not co-parenting well. As other researchers have found, women are much more likely to shoulder the caretaking responsibilities at home; and, just like in my house, this often breeds resentment.

But there are some parents who are getting it right.

Melissa Cronin, a managing director at Accenture, has worked hard to develop a true partnership with her husband. To get to this point, she told me, she has "to consciously recognize the unconscious ways we might otherwise operate." She breaks it down tactically. For example, if their baby wakes up and feels warm, rather than waiting for her husband to tell her their daughter feels warm and ask her what to do, she proactively coaches him, letting him take on some of the responsibility by telling him, "Here's how you decide if we should take her to the hospital."

Melissa also recognizes that maintaining a truly collaborative co-parenting relationship means she can't just be delegating tasks "because, ultimately, then I still have all of that weight on my shoulders. There need to be things that I don't even need to think about, because he is carrying them. Otherwise, there's just too much to think about."

And finally, Melissa, like Shellye Archambeau and so many other successful moms who are thriving, said she relinquishes control. "So that if they don't do it as well as I would, it's okay. It's not the end of the world. Everything will be fine."

If we empower dads, and people of all genders, to show up for parenthood I believe we will all be better than fine. Potentially, much better.

Chapter Six

During a playdate at the home of a family we'd known since Clare was an infant, while the parents gathered in the kitchen and caught up with each other, the kids ran around the huge backyard. Because Grace was almost one and very mobile, I tried to occupy her inside the house so I could join the adult conversation, but she would often drag me outside to help her navigate around the big kids' play.

While I watched Grace climb the hill covered with ivy, and slide down the plastic toy structure, I kept my ear cocked toward the adults. I was listening to the other parents through the screen door when five-year-old Clare tugged on my arm to get my attention. "Suzie says she doesn't want me to be here," she said.

I kissed the top of Clare's head where the blond part revealed her scalp, and said, "Oh, I'm sure she doesn't mean it." And then I turned my attention back to the adults in the house.

An hour later, I was up on the hill in front of the yurt chasing after Grace, when I heard the other kids tell Clare, "Don't look in here. Go away." They were inside the yurt with the door shut, and Clare had been standing outside trying to look in through the plastic drape covering the window. But now, after being told to go away, she was facing me, her face growing red as a dazed smile flashed across her lips. I felt like I had been slapped.

The incidents of the past hour—Clare wandering in and out of the house while the other kids remained outside; Clare sitting alone in the corner; Clare pulling on my arm when I was focused on the other parents; me brushing her off—all coalesced in my mind.

One of the kids opened the door they'd locked to prevent Clare from coming into the yurt and they all ran out. "Don't follow us," they yelled to Clare. "We don't want you with us."

Stunned, I watched as this played out over the next several moments, with Clare stumbling after the kids and them running away from her, chanting, "We don't want you here. We don't want you here."

I grew hot with rage and shame. Fierce thoughts volleyed in my head. Didn't Clare know that she should be ignoring them? That following after them for their approval and affection was feeding their meanness? Was weak? Didn't she have any self-esteem? Didn't she value herself enough not to put up with that? What had I done wrong as her mother? As I stood watching Clare's teeth glint in the sun while her embarrassed smile pushed up the reddening flesh of her cheeks, the thoughts in my head continued to ricochet, gaining speed and volume while becoming increasingly harsh. *This is the way it will always be. Clare's pathetic, just like me. This is the truth of things.*

Through tears I tried to hide, I packed up all of our things and ushered the kids out the door. Clare tried to make eye-contact with me as I fastened her seat belt. When I wouldn't look at her, she put her head down and asked me, in a quiet, small voice, "Mommy, why were they being so mean to me?"

I didn't trust myself to say anything. Clare's occasional sniffle as tears streaked down her face was the only sound in the car as we drove home. Once back at the house, I locked myself in the hallway bathroom, wedging myself between the toilet and the shower and ducking my head between my bent knees. I took some deep breaths, while I ignored Grace and Aidan shouting at each other in the living room as they fought over a toy that they both wanted. I couldn't hear Clare, and I didn't know where she had gone. Thankfully, Shane came in from the backyard and took over. I listened as he intervened between Grace and Aidan. Then he came to knock on my door. "You alright?" he asked. "Yeah," I responded in a shaky voice. "I just need a minute. Can you please check on Clare? She had a rough time at the playdate."

Watching the other kids ridicule Clare forced me to reconnect with the little girl I had been and to acknowledge that, in many ways, I was still that little girl. I thought I'd outgrown those days. I thought I was far removed from the third-grader who, during PE, stood at home plate with a bat raised over her head while the kids jeered, "Look at how fat she is. God, she's so ugly. She needs to go on a diet. How could her mom let her wear those pants out of the house?" That day, I'd been wearing a white flowered cardigan and gray stretch pants, and my face was burning. My hair was pulled back in a bun or a ponytail, not protecting me from anyone's sight, not shielding the "fat" flesh on my cheeks as they flushed deeper and deeper shades of red. Back then, the girl leading the assault was the one I sat up at night dreaming of. I fantasized about sleepovers at her house, and how we'd dress up each other's dolls and watch *Grease* and paint our toenails. And how, if only I was thin enough or pretty enough or somehow better, I could earn her friendship, which would feel like an aura of protecting warmth and light.

I had wanted to run away, but I couldn't. I had to stand there and take it. And as the taunting continued, seeming to escalate in volume and ferocity, I started to cry. And I thought of my dad and how he didn't want me either. The few times I had seen him he'd been distant and uninterested. When I had dinner at his house with his new family, his new kids had laughed at me while I knifed two and then three servings of butter onto my noodles. I couldn't taste it, and so I kept adding more. I didn't understand that the butter was unsalted because I'd never had that kind of butter before. But I did understand that my dad's new kids were thin, and I was not; and that they had my dad's love and affection, and I did not. He was in their life and—except for three of four brief visits—not in mine. My young-er-half siblings had continued to laugh at me, looking at each other as they pointed at my plate full of butter. I had put my head down so they wouldn't see the tears in my eyes.

And later, on that baseball field, while the tears fell down my face and the taunting of my third-grade class-mates merged with the memory of my half-siblings' laughter, it all hurt too much. Something snapped inside me. *I will never again let myself feel this way*, I told myself. I swore that I would not allow myself to want anyone who didn't want me. And I forced myself to stop crying.

As an adult remembering these things, slumped on the cracked linoleum floor of my bathroom, with my face red and my heart beating so fast and hard I could hear it in my ears, I felt the hunger of the little girl in me. How I'd yearned for the friendship of the popular girl in my third-grade class, the acceptance of my half-siblings, and the love of my dad. I experienced all over again how much it hurt to long for them. How it hollowed me out. Left me extended and unbalanced. And how hard I'd fallen into self-loathing when my desire was left unmet for too long.

Feeling the presence of the little girl in me who was still, after all these years, in pain, and my daughter, Clare, who was also hurting, I knew I wanted something better for both of us. I thought about all I'd learned since becoming a mom through my own personal experience and from other parents and researchers.

I called out to the wisdom of *The Mother*. I felt her wrap her arms around me and rock me, just like I'd done so many times with my own kids when they were crying. The warmth of her love moved through me, meeting my longing, soothing my pain. Her wisdom hummed to my adult self and to the little girl I had been: *Loving those who don't love you requires great strength and courage. You are strong and courageous. Your love is bigger than the pain of their rejection. You are loved. You are met. You are held. You are not alone.* I rocked myself back and forth, humming the tune that hummed me. *I am loved. I love. I am loved. I love.*

At bedtime that night, I lay in Clare's bed and wrapped my arms around her. I told her I loved her, and then I shared my story with her. We cried together. We cried for the way we'd both been hurt and because hurt, left untended, hardens the heart.

As I looked to research and my conversations with other parents to help me understand my experience, I realized that parenthood was forcing me to change my habitual response to stress. My old pattern of aggressively resisting the feelings I didn't want no longer served me.

Oxytocin is one of the main hormones involved in bonding and in parenting. It's often called the "love hormone" because it's released during childbirth, breastfeeding, skin-to-skin contact, and other forms of physical bonding, like orgasm. Recent research conducted by neuroscientist Ruth Feldman shows that dads—even non-biological ones—who play a primary role in care-taking may be able to produce as much oxytocin as breast-feeding birth mothers.

According to Shellye E. Taylor, a distinguished research professor at the UCLA Social Neuroscience Lab, when these hormones are present, women may be more likely to respond to stress with the impulse to "tend and befriend," rather than to "fight, flight, or freeze." Which, from an evolutionary standpoint, makes a lot of sense. For the vast majority of the time humans have existed on the planet, women have been pregnant, nursing, or otherwise caring for young children. If one of our ancestors with a small child were to fight or flee a situation, Taylor and others have reasoned, their offspring would be much less likely to survive than if they instead chose to reach out to those around them to develop effective, collaborative ways to address the threat to their survival. As a result, over time, women, especially mothers, seem to have developed a different response to stress than men. When faced with a situation that our neurological system experiences as a threat, our instincts may lead us to seek out social support and to care for ourselves as well as those around us rather than to focus only on our individual survival by freezing, engaging in combat, or running away.

It stands to reason that men who activate their parental brain are likely to develop a similar response to stress. As Dr. Feldman says, "In primary caregiving dads you can have the full parental network system activated to its highest volume."

Discovering this research allowed me to see how bonding with my children was changing my biology. It reminded me of the birth process. My initial response to the physical pain had been to tighten up and fight against it. But when I stopped resisting the contractions and relaxed, a host of beneficial hormones—especially oxytocin—flooded through my body, allowing me to experience the pain in a more supported way.

Similarly, on the night when Clare was bullied, after initially fighting against my own feelings, I'd eventually responded to my pain by reaching towards a wisdom greater than my own. And, just like when I'd been in labor, I was supported enough to grow through the experience.

I couldn't go back to the way I had been. But I could stop fighting who I was becoming.

Opening myself up to new ways of being in relationship with myself and with the world around me was creating the conditions necessary for me to grow. During this period of transition, I often felt vulnerable and unstable as I grappled with all of the emotions I was experiencing.

Before Clare was bullied, there had been other times when I'd retreated into the closet in my bedroom to put my head between my legs, inhale through my nose as silently as possible, and will the air to move into my constricted chest. In those moments, I felt too porous.

I'd spent my life using anger to harden myself to hurt or ignoring my own tender feelings. But after becoming a mom, this old way of being in relation to unwanted feelings stopped working. I felt like a walking bullseye with no armor or protection; so many things penetrated me. I was always on high alert, anticipating the next wave of intense emotions.

My biology was changing, and my behavior had to evolve along with it. Like Dr. Taylor said, "When it is operating during times of low stress, oxytocin physiologically rewards those who maintain good social bonds with feelings of well-being. But, when it comes on board during times of high social stress or pain, it may lead people to seek out more and better social contacts." In reaching out to those who had found their way through similar transformations, who'd crossed from one way of being into another, I began to see how my experience with the anxiety that came from feeling so vulnerable could lead to exponential growth.

Cheryl Porro's story is a good example.

For most of her early years, Cheryl styled herself a rebel. She was drawn to all things off-limits. She cut class to smoke cigarettes beneath the bleachers in the back of her Catholic high school; joined a punk band; became a kick boxer before it was cool; and, because no one thought someone like her—the boy-crazy daughter of a hairdresser—was smart enough, she enrolled in a prestigious university to study chemical engineering. "I was going for the shock factor," Cheryl told me. "No one expected that from me. And I wanted to surprise the hell out of them."

Cheryl said she'd felt fierce, invincible even. Until she got married. And then she started to experience anxiety. Being married made Cheryl feel vulnerable in a way that was new and uncomfortable. She was no longer the outsider smugly looking at all the people on the inside. Now on the inside of a marriage, she felt exposed and susceptible to all of the soft things she'd been immune to before. When Cheryl became a mother, her anxiety escalated. Now she was really on the inside—not just of a partnership, but of a family. A family she'd chosen and created out of her own—once solitary and seemingly invincible, but now tender and vulnerable—body.

For several years after Cheryl became a mom, she dealt with her anxiety by working long hours. She gained weight. She wore jeans and hoodies and settled into what she called "the frumpy mom era," during which she took care of everyone around her but herself.

One day, after she spent thirty minutes writing and rewriting an email to the parents at the preschool where her daughter was scheduled to start, she realized that she didn't even know herself anymore. She was so paralyzed with concern over what others thought of her that she couldn't find her own voice. Rather than the invincible young woman she'd once been, she was now fretting over the language in an email to preschool parents. How, she wondered, had this happened? And, more importantly, how could she reclaim her sense of self? Cheryl committed to unearthing herself.

She began working with a nutritionist, a personal trainer, and eventually, after she'd slimmed and strengthened her body, a personal stylist, who took her shopping and helped her select clothes, accessories, hair styles, and makeup that reflected who she was becoming. Rather than the invincible young rebel, or the "frumpy mom" she had been, Cheryl discovered that her years of feeling raw, tender, and anxious had actually prepared her to be an effective leader.

"What became so clear and apparent to me was how much capacity I had to evolve as a human being," Cheryl said. "And that this evolution came as a result of my leaning into the pain I was feeling and working through it. It was such an awakening for me, that I want to share what I learned with anyone who will listen! Now when someone is open and vulnerable with me about their struggles, I am compelled to do the same and share my own story of transformation. Our greatest strength lies in meeting the truth of our feelings."

Through her experience grappling with her own intense feelings, Cheryl had developed the capacity to nurture others, too. For instance, Cheryl was once managing a transgender woman who was really struggling. If she didn't improve her performance, Cheryl knew she'd have to let her go. At a one-on-one meeting where they were supposed to be talking about technology architecture, Cheryl could tell that this woman was really upset about something. So Cheryl pushed aside their original agenda and asked her to share all that was going on for her. She was underpaid but was not going to get a raise because she was having a hard time communicating effectively with the team. And she was desperate for money because she needed to finish the surgeries to complete her gender transition. And she wanted to grow in her career but she didn't feel like anyone would help her. After Cheryl had listened to all that she had to share, she thanked her for her vulnerable honesty and said: "I can't change what happened in the past. I can only influence what happens in the future. I will commit to you that I will help you. But you need to show up for me. You need to hear my feedback and take it in. And if you will be there for me, I will be there for you every step of the way." Because Cheryl had changed so much, she knew it was possible for others to do the same. She understood that we all have the capacity to transform. And sometimes there needs to be a catalyst of some sort, a person or a moment, to wake us up to our potential. To develop trust with this employee, Cheryl shared instances from her own past that mortified her: such as the time she'd threatened bodily harm to one of her co-workers during a large meeting and was told that she would be escorted from the premises by the police if she ever did anything like that again. Over the course of the next eight to nine months, Cheryl's employee became one of the highest performers in her department, earned a huge pay raise, and eventually left the company to pursue her dream job at a very lucrative salary. "I can't think you enough for what you did for me," she recently said to Cheryl, "I wouldn't be where I am today if it wasn't for you."

As Cheryl's own confidence grew, and her ability to both hire and manage diverse teams who performed well together under her leadership became apparent, she was promoted into the executive ranks within her company. At the time that I interviewed her, she was a Senior Vice President at Salesforce.org, and she's currently the CTO of Curve Health. In 2017, Cheryl was named one of the most powerful female engineers in America by *Business Insider*.

Cheryl's experience of transforming her anxiety into an asset in her life and in her career mirrored that of many other parents I interviewed.

Mart Bailey, the President of Callaway Equity Partners, told me how reading bedtime stories to his daughter forced him to confront the uncomfortable feelings he'd spent his life avoiding. "Each time we get to a certain point in a book where there's sadness," Mart told me, "my daughter really leans into that and wants to know more. And my impulse had been to move on, to distract her. I didn't know when the sadness might stop, it could get out of control. My parents never cried. I learned early on that crying was never okay, I was taught to bury it."

But then one night while Mart was reading to his daughter, she encountered a moment of sadness and started to cry, and rather than distract her, he just held her. Which led her to cry harder and longer.

"It was hard for me," Mart said. "But I knew it was important. I began to realize that you can't just smash it down and push it down. Or, at least, I didn't want to do that anymore with my daughter."

Chapter Seven

Janet Van Huysse had been employee number eighty at Twitter. As their original Vice President of Human Resources and then their Vice President of Diversity and Inclusion, Janet had started some ground-breaking programs for working parents. Her efforts had earned Twitter the reputation as one of the best places for parents to work.

I'd first met Janet when I was five months pregnant with Grace and still working with #YesWeCode. Initially, she had intimidated me. For many years, she'd been the only female executive at Twitter, and she was beautiful in what appeared to be an easy, effortless way. As our first meeting progressed, I mentioned that I was pregnant with my third—and accidental—child. She shared that she'd recently returned from maternity leave after the birth of her third—and also accidental— child. "She's actually made our lives better and easier," Janet said. "What?" I asked. "Is that even possible?" She touched my upper arm with her hand, looked me in the eye and nodded. "Yes," she said. "It's true. And it's possible for you, too."

Back then, I'd been struck by her thoughtful solidarity. So I reached out to her after I'd begun interviewing parents in earnest because I wanted to learn more about her journey, and because I sensed that she could play a critical role in not only furthering my understanding, but in helping me build something with the wisdom I was unearthing.

We sat down over salads in a white, sun-filled lunchroom at Twitter and I told her that our third child hadn't yet made our lives easier. But she had made them infinitely better. She'd been the catalyst for my current quest. And it was a worthy one. I was quieting the demons that had haunted me and developing a deep appreciation for parenthood's potential to further my growth.

I told her about the interviews I'd been conducting with working parents, and how her name had surfaced more than once as a Human Resources leader who was "pioneering" on behalf of parents at Twitter. What, I asked, had she done to earn such a reputation?

Janet was the first person at Twitter to go out on maternity leave, so she'd created their first policy—for herself. As more women at the company began having babies, she formed a quarterly roundtable for moms who were preparing for or returning from leave. These sessions initially began as logistical meetings to help the women file their paperwork but quickly became much more. Not only did they create a community of support among the women going through the life-changing experience of becoming mothers, these meetings also served as a powerful feedback loop for Janet. Through these conversations, she learned about the challenges moms at her company were facing, and then she took steps to address them. When she discovered that many mothers were struggling with pumping breast milk because it took too much time out of their workday, she installed hospital-grade breast pumps, which are faster, more efficient, and easier to use, in all of the mothers' rooms in all the Twitter offices. When she heard that some women were struggling to find role models who could help them progress in their careers while also starting families, she started a "mommy mentor" program to pair mothers of older children with those who had newborns.

Janet initiated a quarterly roundtable for new fathers as well. When she learned that getting dinner on the table at the end of the day was a logistical challenge most parents would rather not face, she launched a dinner-to-go service to allow all employees to take meals home with them at the end of the day. She started the program because parents had shared the need for it, but she made it available to every employee to avoid alienating anyone who might resent parents for having special access to this benefit.

Janet then created a quarterly roundtable for managers who had new parents on their teams. Working with the managers, Janet told me, was especially important. Far too many of them were alienating the parents on their teams. For instance, when one manager saw one of his direct reports crying on her first day back at work after maternity leave, he attempted to empathize with her by sharing how his wife had struggled with going back to work and had ultimately decided to stay home with their kids. "Now she plays tennis all of the time and she's much happier," he told the crying mother. This new mom on his team, who was her family's only breadwinner and the highest performer in their large department, felt both offended and alienated. She shared during the quarterly roundtable that Janet hosted for moms that her manager's comments made her feel as though he didn't have confidence in her ability to perform now that she was a mom.

After telling me about her work for parents at Twitter, Janet asked me to detail more of what I was learning in my interviews. I explained that while everyone arrived at parenthood with their own unique set of challenges, it was becoming apparent that there was a specific set of skills that parenthood helped develop. And these skills were interconnected.

At its core, parenthood forces us to become intimate—first with our infant, then with ourselves, and, ultimately, with the world around us. To attune ourselves to the needs of our infant we must develop new levels of perception. And in the process of doing this, we must continually shed any blocks that would prevent us from being fully present with the truth of the moment.

When we continue to show up for parenthood—*really* show up—we access new ways of being in the world.

I told Janet that more than 80% of all of the parents I interviewed reported developing an enhanced capacity in five core areas: emotional intelligence, courage, purpose, efficiency and productivity, and the ability to collaborate.

After I'd finished, Janet sat quietly, gazing across the room. After a few minutes, she looked up at me and said, "The companies who will succeed in the twenty-first century will be the ones who recognize that parents are an asset to their organization. The skills acquired by parenting are the same skills they need in their leaders."

I felt like I'd been doused in cold water. My body tingled with the implications of what she'd said. Could Janet be right? Were the skills developed while parenting valuable—critical even—in the modern workplace?

I decided to look into it.

The World Economic Forum's "The Future of Jobs Report 2018" indicates that the skills required to perform most jobs are changing. Uniquely human skills, such as those developed while parenting, are becoming increasingly valuable.

As automation continues to replace roles formerly held by people, many of the remaining positions will be those only humans can fill. Dentons, the largest law firm in the world, recognizes that technology is disrupting their industry. Attorney Maya Markovich, a mom I interviewed, is the head of product at NextLaw Labs, an innovation program run by Dentons to help them shape and drive the changes brought about by technology. Much of her work focuses on anticipating how technology will impact the legal industry—and the role humans will occupy in the legal realm in the future.

As Maya explained to me, technology—and artificial intelligence in particular—is gaining traction in the legal world. It's beginning to affect a significant amount of work now done by lawyers, particularly the more onerous, repetitive activities that require minimal analysis and do not significantly improve the quality of the service provided. According to Maya, "As this sixteenth-century guild adapts to the mandates of the twenty-first century, traditional legal skills are fast becoming table stakes, and a larger cultural shift is afoot. Inclusiveness, emotional intelligence, and empathy are increasingly valuable skills that will define most successful lawyers of the future. These abilities will enable them to focus on higher value work, strategic and creative thinking, and issues that demand insight and strong collaborative skills. They will also produce better results, higher revenues, and more satisfied clients."

This doesn't just apply to the law; technology is disrupting nearly every industry. And as this continues to increase at an exponential rate, virtually all companies, organizations, and businesses are becoming technology companies.

Also, work is becoming increasingly team based. When people work in teams, research shows they are happier and more productive. This is because collaboration, according to game theorist Martin Nowak, is always the most successful form of engagement. A world-renowned professor, Nowak says Darwin was wrong: collaboration, not competition, is the key to survival. In the long run, cooperators, those who work well with others, are the ones most likely to win anywhere—in the animal kingdom, in computer simulations, and even in corporate environments.

Armed with this understanding, in 2012, Google launched Project Aristotle, an ambitious study to determine the optimal conditions for team productivity. After reviewing all of the academic studies looking at how teams worked, and scrutinizing the work of hundreds of Google's teams, the researchers concluded that psychological safety, more than any other factor, served as the foundation for a team's ability to succeed.

That conclusion led them to look further into Harvard Business School professor Amy Edmondson's 1999 paper which defined psychological safety as a "shared belief held by members of a team that the team is safe for interpersonal risk-taking . . . [It is] a sense of confidence that the team will not embarrass, reject or punish someone for speaking up." This means that team members can admit mistakes, learn from failure, and openly share ideas, which can lead to improved decision-making and innovation.

The Google employees working on Project Aristotle—a mix of researchers, statisticians, organizational psychologists, sociologists, and engineers—set out to determine how they could translate all that they'd learned about psychological safety, and the conditions necessary to create it, into actionable guidelines accessible to all Google employees. And, because they are Google, they wanted to know how they could do it with increasing speed, precision, and effectiveness. In their study of 180 employee teams, they found that the way teammates treated one another was more important than anything else, including group composition, motivation, or level of education.

Some of the ways successful teams exhibited care for each other included having equal talk time or "conversational turn-taking," and high levels of applied empathy, or "social sensitivity," which means that members were skilled at understanding others through nonverbal cues.

Other research conducted by Daniel Goleman, who co-directs the Consortium for Research on Emotional Intelligence in Organizations at Rutgers University and is one of our leading experts on emotional intelligence, has found that beyond a certain point, there is little or no correlation between an individual's IQ and their professional success. Instead, emotional intelligence accounts for nearly 90% of what moves people up the ladder when IQ and technical skills are roughly similar.

When it comes to teams, other studies have found that taking time to develop organic group norms— which both create high levels of psychological safety and allow for individual team members to grow over time—are highly effective at leading to success.

Project Aristotle also revealed that encouraging people to be honest about some of their most vulnerable feelings accelerates the adoption of the practices which lead to optimal performance. In other words, being honest about our feelings—first with ourselves, and then with each other—likely unlocks a team's ability to work well together.

Chapter Eight

It took months, but I eventually convinced Janet to join me in co-founding a business devoted to helping companies realize parenthood's positive potential in the workplace. We met on Tuesdays over lattes to build the first model for our business, which we named TendLab. We sought the counsel of other leaders in the space, like Sarah Roos-Essl, who had been the leader of Twitter's parents' group, and a powerful advocate for change inside Twitter; Natalie Miller, a data scientist with an incredible background as employee eleven at Instacart and the founder of her own tech startup, Doxa, which worked to address bias in the workplace; Erica Priggen-Wright, a marketing, branding, and storytelling expert who has launched several successful public campaigns for mission-oriented ventures; and Lucy Farey-Jones, a single mom and the only female co-founder of one of the top ten ad agencies in the United States.

With the wisdom of these advisors and others, my research, and Janet's many years of experience, we initially designed TendLab as a boutique consulting firm committed to helping companies meaningfully address parenthood at work.

We didn't anticipate how painful and emotionally-charged discussing parenthood at work would be for almost everyone—not just parents. Or how holding the space for people to share their feelings would bring so much to the surface. Parenthood at work, I discovered, was the entry point to deeper issues.

I was initially shocked by how many people showed up to our optional sessions. With the first company we worked with, for instance, more than 75% of all employees attended our one-and-a-half-hour presentation on parenthood's potential to have a positive impact on career performance.

During our talk, I first detailed the career-critical skills parenthood can unlock. I outlined the main themes that emerged in the interviews I had conducted with high-performing parents. I then detailed the research from other disciplines, like neuroscience and evolutionary biology, which further validated what I'd found in my interviews. In the second half of the presentation, Janet explained why the skills developed while parenting are not only relevant—but essential— in the twenty-first century workplace.

At the end of the presentation, Janet and I thought we'd be greeted with loud applause. We weren't. People clapped, but not much. In general, the people in the audience looked uncomfortable.

I remember the shift within me at that moment. How I pushed the hair I'd blown straight that morning behind my ears, let out the mom-pooch that I'd been sucking in, and took a deep breath. It was time to get real. Walking away from the front of the room and out into the audience, I encouraged people to speak up.

"Be honest," I said. "Tell us what this brought up for you. It's the only way forward."

There was a long silence. And then it began. One woman stood up to say that our presentation invalidated the reasons she'd chosen not to have children. She said she expected her career to progress faster than her female colleagues who were mothers and that she'd consciously given up having a family after she'd seen how motherhood worked against ambitious women. A mother who suffered from postpartum depression said our talk didn't reflect her experience or acknowledge the significant challenges she continued to face as a working mom. As she shared, tears streaming down her face, people nodded, clapped, and shouted words of encouragement. And then it took off, and many people opened up about how and why our presentation didn't speak to the truth of their experience of parenthood at work.

When we were preparing for the presentation, we decided not to talk about the challenges working parents face. Everyone already knows how hard it is, we had reasoned. So, we'd only included one slide that highlighted the discrimination both moms and dads who appear to have caregiving responsibilities are likely to face at work. The rest of our presentation focused on the benefits of parenthood.

However, in not fully acknowledging how much people were suffering, our message wasn't complete.

And I've since learned that people don't trust what we're saying unless we share the *whole* truth.

Now when I work inside companies, I talk about shame first. Before anything else, I make a point of discussing the pain that is a part of parenthood and work today. I share that in the hundreds of interviews I conducted, almost every single working parent admitted that they were suffering. We all feel as though we are falling short of our ideals at work or at home—or both. I also discuss how people without kids often resent their co-workers with kids, even—and especially—when they can't say this out-loud. It is also critical, I've found, to acknowledge that there may be people in the audience who wanted children but who—for a variety of reasons, such as infertility, pregnancy-related challenges, or the heart-wrenching loss of a child—do not have them.

Acknowledging this and putting it up front in our presentations and workshops, creates the space for people to be honest with themselves and each other in an environment that does not usually allow for the expression of these truths. This part of the process didn't fit into our neat picture of how we initially thought our engagements would unfold. Unearthing raw feelings is messy. But it is the deep work that precedes any real change. And even though, at first, I wasn't sure where it would take us, I knew it was necessary to allow people to share their vulnerable, raw, and tender parts—the regions that for far too long have gone un-tended.

Amy Henderson

Up until now, Western culture has identified the "ideal worker" as someone with no domestic responsibilities who uses their intellect in order to compete their way to the top. This "ideal worker," a term coined by sociologists, is essentially a straight, white man who has a stay-at-home wife to tend to his kids and domestic needs so that he can be fully devoted to his career. Even though more than 80% of American workers today don't have a stay-at-home partner, our workplaces are still designed for this conception of the "ideal worker."

We assert in all TendLab presentations that this "ideal worker" is not the optimal performer in today's workplace. Our sessions make the strong case that caretaking—especially parenthood—has value, that it can lead to the development of skills that are not only relevant, but critical, for success in the modern workplace. And because this goes against almost everything we've been trained to believe, it often cracks people open and forces them to reckon with all the ways they've forsaken their relationships with themselves and others to progress on their professional trajectories.

Once we realized that talking about parenthood at work was an emotionally-charged topic for almost everyone, we designed our presentations to use this pain as a portal. When we hold the space for people to be honest with themselves and each other, these conversations become an entry point to working together to design a better future.

We allow people without kids to express their rage and resentment. To be honest when they feel as though their own needs—to leave on time; have off-time during the weekends; not be tasked with last-minute, inconvenient trips—were less credible than the needs of their colleagues who were parents.

We encourage parents to experience their full range of emotions, too. For some, our presentation heightens the already intense feelings of guilt they experience. While it may be slightly more acceptable for them to set limits at work, parenthood often feels as though it is in direct conflict with their careers. That is, because of their careers, they are all too often forced to miss out on parenthood. It is not uncommon for people to sob as they talk about getting to see their kids for only a few minutes during a workday, if at all, and how, during these small windows of time, they were stressed and rushed, trying to feed and bathe and otherwise meet the physical needs of their kids. This left them feeling like they had little to no time left for the tender, oxytocin-inducing bonding that causes many of the beneficial neurological changes we'd outlined.

A woman on track to make partner at Goldman Sachs told me, "My kids get the dregs of me. When I come home at the end of the day, if I even make it in time to see my kids, I am usually worn out and exhausted because I've already given the best of myself to my work." The bottom line is that many parents all too often prioritize their careers over their relationships with their kids. For many of these parents, our presentation can feel like salt in an already open wound within them.

For many people, not having children is a source of grief. And we've learned that it is essential to create workplaces that can acknowledge their suffering.

People who've lost children rarely speak up during our sessions. I had expected this. From the interviews I conducted with parents who had lost children, I understood that the workplace is rarely capable of handling the truth of their experience. A woman who'd lost her full-term baby when she was only twenty-four-hours-old told me that her return to work was one of the most emotionally triggering experiences. She thought returning to the structure and routine of work would provide her with a sense of safety and comfort. But instead, it was really difficult. "I was different," she said. "And it was so hard for everyone that I worked with to deal with their own horror of what had happened. There were people I passed in the hallway who wouldn't even make eye contact with me. I remember spending a lot of energy trying to appear normal and fine. There were really only a few people who could handle the truth of my experience. My boss, who I imagined would be one of the most supportive, was actually strangely aggressive and cruel. I found that she'd had a similar experience but had never really been able to grieve it. It gave me a much better perspective, and a lot more compassion for her. We still have a lot more work to do in terms of how we deal with grieving as a society."

This mom wasn't alone. Many people who had either lost children or been unable to have them often felt at odds with their co-workers with children. One woman who'd been unable to conceive told me she felt discriminated against when company funds went to finance in-office baby showers. "Where's my sorry-you-can't-be-a-mom cake?" she asked through tears.

Managers and people in leadership positions often respond to our sessions with resistance. For them, even though they can't publicly acknowledge it, parenthood has always been a liability. Whenever someone has a baby, they expect it to be expensive. And while they may want to be supportive and empathetic, they are still accountable for the performance of their team or their company. When someone was out on parental leave and then returned sleep- deprived and distracted by their surging hormones and resultant neurological changes, they assume this will have a negative impact on the success of the organization—until our presentation asks them to consider that it might be otherwise.

Our most impactful work inside companies—the engagements that earn the most positive evaluations from our participants—are our peer-based sessions. When we create the space for people to both share and listen to others about their challenges navigating parenthood and work, it serves to unlock something in both the group and the individuals within it. Just like I discovered during my interviews with individual parents, our ability to recognize how parenthood positively impacts our own development requires us to first acknowledge how much we are struggling. When we are honest with ourselves and each other, when we give voice to the negative thoughts that we've been harboring about ourselves because we aren't doing anything as well as we think we should be in the company of others who do the same, it begins to liberate us. We start to recognize that we are not suffering because we are individually incompetent and incapable, but because we are in impossible situations. When we realize that *we* aren't the problem, we start to free ourselves from the debilitating and dark shame that would keep us mired in it. Then—and only then—can we become an effective part of the solution.

Becoming part of the solution requires us to get to the root of the problem. After spending five years interviewing parents and working with companies to address the impact of parenthood on the workforce, I now recognize the problem: Our workplaces are not designed to recognize the transformative value of care—outside of the office, or inside the office.

Other studies have found that when a man helps his co-workers, it positively impacts his performance evaluation; but if he refuses to help his coworkers, it doesn't negatively impact how he's rated. For a woman, the exact opposite is true: helping others doesn't boost her evaluation; but refusing to help others harms her performance assessment. We found this to be especially true for mothers. In our surveys, focus groups, and interviews, we discovered that mothers, more than any other group, feel as though they are expected to tend to the needs of their co-workers or suffer the consequences. However, despite the expectation that they, as women with children, should care for and nurture their colleagues, they felt as though any time or energy they invested in tending to the needs of their co-workers actually worked against them. Like one mother who had started and led an Employee Resource Group for parents at her large company, reported, "My manager told me he wasn't going to give me the bonus or the promotion I'd earned because I was wasting my time on activities that were outside the scope of my deliverables. But then, when I told him I'd pass off the leadership of the Parent Employee Resource Group he told me he'd demote me to a lesser position within the organization if I didn't maintain the group." This mother, like many others I spoke with inside our client companies, felt as though she was "damned if she helped others, and damned if she didn't."

It's time for us to recognize the transformative power of caring for others—both at home and at work—for people of all genders, whether or not they are parents.

After working inside several companies, we found that each organization has their own specific challenges that must be addressed and strengths which can be built upon. In general, however, the following eleven practices are effective at creating the conditions necessary to build a work culture which values care:

1   Model from the top: show that caring is valued by company leadership
   When leaders show they value caregiving in their own lives—by taking parental leave, setting boundaries around their time so they can be present with their families, being offline between six and eight p.m. so they can be present for family dinner and bedtime, bringing pictures and stories of their families to work—it signals that it's safe for others to do the same.

2   Provide equal parental leave for all parents
   It is important to provide the same parental benefits to all employees regardless of gender, birth status, or the professional level of the employee, not just white-collar workers. Everyone deserves to show up for their families, and to develop the career relevant skills parenthood can unlock.

3   Provide miscarriage leave
   I interviewed way too many mothers who were not offered a single day of leave when they suffered the premature loss of a child or a stillborn birth. You don't need research to explain how and why this is not humane.

4 <u>Provide caregiver and bereavement leave</u>
   When other caregivers, not just parents, are supported in showing up for their families it helps mitigate
   resentment directed towards parents in the workplace. It also signals that all caregiving is valued.
   Allowing employees to take time off so they can ad-
   equately grieve the loss of their loved ones is both
   compassionate and smart. Without the ability to process grief, employee performance is likely to suffer.

5 <u>Be thoughtful about supporting caregivers who</u>
   <u>are going out and returning from leave</u>
   While working with companies, Janet and I discovered the value of empowering parents to create their
   own leave and return plans, especially with the support of their peers. For example, Lori Mihalich-Levin
   has an online course called "Mindful Return" for
   parents returning to work after parental leave. This
   peer-based program, which enables parents to engage deeply with one another in an honest, supportive environment, has had profound results: over 94%
   of parents who take the course are still employed five
   years later; and 85% are still working at the company that paid for them to attend the course.

6 <u>Resource caregivers' co-workers when a caregiver</u>
   <u>goes out on leave</u>
   Use caregiver leave as an opportunity to give that
   caregivers' co-workers more meaningful work. For

one of the first companies we worked with, though money was tight, they could bring in contractors and interns so that the rest of the team could focus their time and energy on strategic, high-level work. Organizations like the Prowess Project, or the Mom Project, can help to temporarily fill the position of a caregiver who is out on leave.

7 <u>Don't assume a one-size-fits-all approach will work</u>
Create the conditions necessary for clear and consistent communication between caregivers and their co-workers, managers, and the HR team. A parent returning from parental leave may want a reduced workload and less critical projects for a window of time when they first come back, or they may not. One mom told me, "If I'm going to leave my kid at home to go to work, I want to do something meaty and meaningful, something that makes it worth the pain of being away from my baby." While some parents or caregivers may not want to travel frequently or take on high-pressure assignments, research shows that many parents are just as likely to want these opportunities as people without kids. One single dad told me, "If I plan ahead, I can secure childcare for my son so that I can travel for work; but I am never offered those assignments. And I feel as though I am not being promoted as quickly as others because I am not considered for these trips."

8 <u>Stay attuned to your caregivers' work experience</u>
When Janet and I were coming up with names for
our business, we had strongly considered "Canary,"
because if parents are struggling to survive in a
workplace, it's probably not a healthy environment
for anyone. And while there are specific things that
apply only to parents—such as having hospital grade
breast pumps in Mothers' Rooms—there are many
things which may disproportionately impact parents,
but which also influence the experience of everyone
else. For instance, one company we worked with
had a very young workforce with many first-time
managers who didn't know how to run effective
meetings. As a result, employees spent most of their
days in meetings that did not help them meet their
deliverables. Parents and caregivers, who had significantly less time than everyone else, suffered the most
because they had to find the time to get their work
done during non-business hours; but everyone was
negatively affected by this ineffective situation.

9 <u>Establish caregiver Employee Resource
Groups (ERGs)</u>
Empower parents and other caregivers to develop
a community of peers for support but be mindful
of the expectations you place on this group. Many
companies ask their ERGs to do a lot of work, like
to on-board parents after leave, play an active role
in recruitment, and coordinate "bring your kids to

work days," without compensating or acknowledging the parents who do this unpaid labor. We recommend employers link engagement with ERGs to performance evaluations and bonuses.

10 <u>Intentionally recruit and hire caregivers</u>
Organizations like PathForward offer paid internships to caregivers returning to work after a career break. You can also list job openings on job sites targeting parents and other caregivers.

11 <u>Have a company-wide policy enabling stigma-free flexible work arrangements</u>
Companies that allow all employees the flexibility they need to do their best work are the best workplaces for caregivers. Significant research indicates that all employees, regardless of their caregiver status, want flexible work arrangements. That can mean anything from working from home on occasion to having flexible working hours.

It is true that caregivers need flexible work arrangements. However, if a company creates a policy where only caregivers are given access to this benefit, either implicitly or explicitly, it is likely to lead to resentment among their teammates and to the marginalization of caregivers. This, in turn, may affect their ability to get promoted and to be seen as valuable, committed parts of their teams. Also, because caregivers already face significant bias in the workplace,

I found that individuals who are further marginalized may disproportionately suffer when companies do not explicitly allow all employees to have flexible work arrangements.

i. I first noticed this when I interviewed a single mother of color who, despite her stellar career performance which had led to her being promoted three times over her two-year tenure at her company, had never taken a day off of work to show up for her kids. She'd missed every parent-teacher conference, sporting event, and extra-curricular activity that took place during business hours. As she understood it, being the sole breadwinner for her kids meant that she couldn't afford to do anything that might jeopardize her career. In contrast, all of the mostly white dads I interviewed at that same company, many of whom had wives at home, hadn't missed any of their kids' activities. Since they weren't facing additional layers of bias, like the single mom of color, they felt secure enough to take off as much time as they wanted.

ii. A landmark 2010 study at Best Buy's corporate headquarters found that when employees were evaluated only on their results and not on the amount of time they were in the office or the number of hours that they worked, it significantly reduced work and family conflict without reducing employee productivity. This intervention empowered all employees to take control of their time and enabled everyone, not just caregivers, to succeed. It also eliminated the "flexibility" stigma caregivers were likely to face if they took advantage of policies that were only available to them.

If you are leading a company, this might seem like a lot. You don't have to do everything at once, but prioritizing your parents and caregivers is an incredibly valuable way to improve the quality of your workplace—for everyone. Taking any step is one in the right direction.

Chapter Nine

The sun was pink in a gray, dirty sky as I drove to meet with evolutionary biologist Dr. Sarah Blaffer-Hrdy at her farm in Northern California. It was November of 2018 and California was experiencing its deadliest wildfire on record. This fire, and the others that had preceded it in recent years, would soon be cited in a major U.S. report as just one of many of the devastating effects of climate change. The report concludes that "earth's climate is now changing faster than at any point in the history of modern civilization, primarily as a result of human activities."

I am meeting with Sarah Hrdy because I am hopeful that she can help me finish this book. In an earlier chapter, I've written about much of her pioneering work. On this day, as I drive past drivers with gas masks on their faces, I'm eager to talk about her discovery that our ancestors shared the care of their young, which led to the emergence of altruistic, or prosocial tendencies, and how this altered our minds and enabled us to become the complex, advanced society we are today.

Over iced tea in her large farmhouse, I tell her how much her work has helped me. Particularly her discovery that human altruism is rooted in our ancestral mothers' willingness to have multiple loving and nurturing caretakers for their kids. This liberated me from an enormous amount of guilt. And it gave me permission to embrace a larger community of caretakers for my kids. Like I told her, I now know that my kids and I are both better off if I'm not the only one caring for them.

While we're seated across from each other, I ask Sarah, "What was the catalyst for our ancient ancestors to become communal in the care of their young?"

"The main predisposing condition is environmental challenges," she tells me. "It all comes down to food security."

A million light bulbs go off in my head, and for a moment, I am almost unable to breathe.

Environmental challenges leading to reduced food security is not an abstract concept for me. I'd been a Peace Corps volunteer in Malawi, East Africa during the AIDS pandemic during which time there was also a severe climate change-related drought that led to massive starvation.

Sarah's seated figure becomes blurry as my mind flashes back to one of the most traumatic incidents I encountered. The scene was so painful that it took me many months of therapy and other healing work to even remember all that had occurred. After coming back to the U.S., I worked with trauma therapists specializing in EMDR, Eye Motion Desensitization and Reprocessing, where binaural stimulation allowed me to access the incidents, like this one, which haunted me the most. While my therapist tapped back and forth on my right and left knee, which alternately simulated the right and left side of my brain, I could unlock the memories my mind had hidden from me. And when I was back in the scenes, reliving them in fleshed out details which I shared out loud, I found that I could eventually alter the way I processed them.

For instance, through EMDR, I spent several sessions going back to this particular day when I'd run away from the mothers with malnourished babies.

Left knee tap. Right knee tap. Left knee tap.
Right knee tap.

I remembered how the fierce sun dried my sweat into salty trails down my face, neck, and back. And how my head pounded as I adjusted my blue and white palm tree sun visor to look out at the quarter-mile long line of mothers in brightly colored sarong skirts. My eyes watered, the view before me wavering like a mirage, as I took in the many babies. Most of the babies were carried on their mother's backs, in cloth slings that crossed between their bare breasts, which hung flat like pancakes with raisin nipples. But some infants were swaddled in cocoons of cloth nestled in the nooks of their mother's necks or in the crooks of their arms. And when the women came up, one at a time, to unwrap their infants and hold them out to the two health care workers, Mercy and Mrs. Kuzimva, the babies were generally assessed by only one measurement: a crude hanging scale.

Left knee tap. Right knee tap. Left knee tap.
Right knee tap.

When removed from the warmth of their mothers, some of the babies, healthy and plump, belted out hearty cries. These women were shouted at in Chichewa by Mercy or Mrs. Kuzimva, "Your baby is fine. Stop wasting my time," And they were waved away.

Left knee tap. Right knee tap. Left knee tap.
Right knee tap.

Other babies had moon-shaped heads, swollen ankles and feet, distended bellies. Their peeling skin flaked off like fish food, falling to the ground in brittle white flecks as they were transferred to the cloth scale. These babies were suffering from a lack of protein, otherwise known as Kwashiorkor, which can cause organ failure and brain damage and is life-threatening if left untreated. But their mothers didn't always receive the two heaping scoops of government issued soy-corn flour. The rules specified that only low-weight babies should receive food. And these swollen infants, whose black hair often had a reddish tint, usually weighed a normal, even above average, weight for their ages. So it was a judgment call. And from where I stood—behind Mercy and Mrs. Kuzimva, busying myself with hauling forward and ripping open the bags of flour—it seemed arbitrary. I wasn't an expert, but it looked as though some of the most swollen babies were turned away.

Left knee tap. Right knee tap. Left knee tap.
Right knee tap.

Other babies were bird-like, skeletal, and well below the weight for their ages. Their tiny bones—skulls, ribs, knuckles—often loomed large inside their taut flesh. Their mothers always received food. And a lecture. Sometimes Mercy, but always Mrs. Kuzimva, raised their arms and shouted in Chichewa as loud as they could, "Your baby is starving. You must feed your baby. Do you hear me?"

Left knee tap. Right knee tap. Left knee tap.
Right knee tap.

The women almost always responded by bending their knees and rounding their heads and shoulders to the ground in submission. Their faces, blank and stoic, stared at the hard, parched earth while they held out their cloth bags to receive their two scoops of coarsely ground soy-corn flour. We'd been passing out the government rations every few weeks for several months, and I was struck by how almost every mother would bow low, her eyes still on the ground, to whisper, *zikomo, zikomo* (thank you, thank you) before she walked away.

Left knee tap. Right knee tap. Left knee tap.
Right knee tap.

I understood why Mercy and Mrs. Kuzimva, who earned a monthly salary of around $20 USD and were just barely insulated from starvation, were harsh with the mothers. It was how they'd been trained to cope with the situation, and how they distanced themselves from the role they had to play. But that day, because we knew we didn't have enough flour for everyone who qualified, Mrs. Kuzimva was especially punitive. Flecks and strands of her white spit rained down on the women as she screamed at them. "What kind of mother are you?" "How could you not feed your child?" and "What is wrong with you?"

Left knee tap. Right knee tap. Left knee tap.
Right knee tap.

We'd only gone through about one-fourth of the line when Mrs. Kuzimva reached her breaking point. She turned to me and said in heavily accented English, "You. Now. Here." She motioned for me to take her place. I stepped forward as she slipped behind me. Mercy also moved back. "Yes, Amy. Your turn," she agreed, her face stern.

And then it was just me in front of the mothers. I'd never been in front before. Never been the one who had to decide.

Left knee tap. Right knee tap. Left knee tap.
Right knee tap.

Sitting in the therapist's office, my pulse exploded in my chest as sweat dripped down my face and armpits. I flashed my eyes open and stood up. "That's it. That's as far as I can go today."

In addition to working with a series of skilled EMDR therapists, I also became an apprentice to a Lakota Sundancer. At least once a week, we engaged in some type of ceremony, and I was particularly grateful for the sweat lodges. In a backyard in a complex of track homes in West Marin, we sat together in a "womb" of burlap blankets hung over arching, inter-connected birch branches. During the ceremony, the "fire-keeper" outside shoveled hot stones, which were called "grand-mothers," inside to the "water pourer," who placed them in a pit in the center of the circle. He splashed water onto the stones and the heat rose to flush our bodies red while he led us in rounds of prayer and song. In the thick, sweaty darkness, surrounded by others who were intent on their own words and the longings beneath them, I felt free to whisper in feverish spurts, "Please help me. I don't know who I am anymore. I'm surrounded by family and friends who love me, but I feel so foreign and strange. How do I stop hating my-self? And them? I feel so heavy and dark all of the time. I want to believe that I can do or be something useful, meaningful, positive. But sometimes I wonder if that's just naive and childish. Help me believe again."

When someone was really suffering—after a miscar-riage, or after their spouse had left them—the water pourer kept them in the lodge for an extra round after everyone else had stepped out. I'd been a part of the community for about four months when I was instruct-ed to remain inside for a fifth, private round. "You can't carry it all. You must let it go," the water pourer instructed me as we sat in the dark and he doused the stones, again and again and again, with water. As the scalding steam filled the space around us, I opened my mouth wide like a fish gasping out of water. I couldn't breathe. And then something in me released—something I didn't even know I'd been holding onto—and I started to sob. Loud wrenching wails worked their way out of me, moving from my gut up through my chest and throat in peristaltic pushes that hurt so good.

Covered in sticky phlegm and sweat and tears, I emerged from the lodge what felt like hours or months or even years later, even though that extra round had probably only lasted about thirty minutes. I walked away from the group, stepped outside the knee-length wood fence surrounding the yard, and stood for some time in my saturated, floor-length cotton dress. Swaying and blinking up at the sun, which had never looked so bright, I felt ageless and timeless, both very old and incredibly young and everything in between. And then I passed out.

At my next EMDR session, we went back to the line of waiting mothers.

Left knee tap. Right knee tap. Left knee tap.
Right knee tap.

Before me was a slight woman named Amayi Sokho, whom I knew by name because she sometimes sold "chippies," or fried potatoes, at the Tuesday market in our village. I motioned her forward and she showed me her sleeping infant. Her knees held my attention. They were much too large, a massive joint stuck between two tinker toy sticks that should've been legs. But they couldn't be legs because no child could walk or stand or even exist with such impossibly tiny sticks for legs.

Left knee tap. Right knee tap. Left knee tap.
Right knee tap.

I took a long, deep breath and nodded to the mother, *Yes, your child needs food.* With the plastic shovel, I heaved two large scoops, more than the other women received, into her bag. I did not look at Amayi Sokho. I did not look at the child. When I was finished, before she'd sealed her bag shut, I turned and walked away.

Left knee tap. Right knee tap. Left knee tap.
Right knee tap.

Behind me, Amayi Sokho muttered her "Zikomo. Zikomo." Mrs. Kazembe shouted, "Where are you going? We are not done." And Mercy yelled, too, "Amy, come back. We still have food to give away here."

Left knee tap. Right knee tap. Left knee tap.
Right knee tap.

But I did not turn back. I did not answer.

I walked directly to my cement house with its peeling blue and white paint and corrugated tin roof. It was only 600 feet away, but it seemed to take forever to get there. Once inside, I used duct tape to hang two cloths over my windows, securing all of the edges so that no one could see inside. Then I dug into my duffel bag and took out the cardboard box my grandmother had sent me. In the box were ten packages of Reese's peanut-butter cups, a bag of Hershey's Miniatures chocolates, four bags of Pepperidge Farm Goldfish crackers, and a bag of Fritos.

Left knee tap. Right knee tap. Left knee tap.
Right knee tap.

In my therapist's office, I wanted to open my eyes and stop the scene. But I took a deep breath and continued.

Back in Malawi, I tucked the box and myself into the reed mat bed under my mosquito net and buried my entire body in my red North Face sleeping bag. Cocooned and sweating in nylon and polyester, with only a tiny circle of light above my head, I ate all the food in the box.

With my eyes still closed, and in a voice thick with phlegm, I told my therapist, "I don't know what to do now." Tears dampened my quivering chin.

"What do you need?" she asked.

"I need to pretend that none of this happened. And that I'm still the good, kind person I thought I was."

"What if it wasn't you? What if it was someone else, someone you loved, who'd been in your place? What would you say to them?"

I swallowed. I didn't want to play along with her or answer her questions. I swallowed again. I rubbed my hands up and down my legs. "I guess I would tell her that it did happen. But there wasn't much she could've done. And yet I know that's not entirely true. She could've shared her food. She could've raised money to buy more food. She could've done a million things other than walk away and hide."

"Can you see how she's hurting because she cares so much. And that she's far away from home for the first time and overwhelmed and not prepared to handle the situation?"

"Yeah, I guess so."

"Can you forgive her for not being, in that moment, the very best possible person she could've been?"

"Maybe," I said, my voice small, barely audible. "Maybe someday"

Eventually, my body rigid with the memory I've just re-lived, Sarah Hrdy's form starts to come back into focus. I see that she's looking at me with a curious, kind smile. And I have no idea how long I've been disconnected from our conversation.

But I find comfort in Sarah's presence, and in the wisdom she has spent a lifetime acquiring. She believes that humans are, by nature, an altruistic species. And I now know this altruism traces back approximately 2.6 million years to when we faced drastic environmental challenges. Her groundbreaking research illuminates how those of us who survived—and who gave birth to offspring who survived—were the ones who banded together to care for one another's young during long ago times where food was scarce because the earth was rapidly changing.

Evolutionary Anthropologist Richard Lee's work asserts that the drastically changing environment our surviving ancestors faced caused them to collaborate in many ways, not just in the care of their young. They lived in hunter-gatherer societies where they traveled long distances to barter for goods among both close and distant kin and non-relatives. During this time, our ancestors' willingness to invest in the well-being of those around them, to be generous in sharing their resources, enhanced their ability to survive. If they shared the animal they killed in a hunt, the goodwill they created with others would make them more likely to be given harvested berries and nuts when they were hungry and without food. Because of this, developing and maintaining good relationships with others mattered. A lot. Our main form of engagement within our communities and with strangers was cooperation, not competition. And war and fighting were relatively infrequent.

It was only about 10,000 years ago, when we became an agrarian society and stopped roaming the land and began to settle, that we began to change the way we related to those who were not close kin. When we claimed ownership over land resources, fighting became more common. Competition, rather than cooperation, eventually became the dominant form of engagement between communities. As corporations came into existence and we progressed into the industrial era, machines and factories became more important than land, and we continued to compete and fight over controlling these means of production.

Now, however, in the age of information, data is eclipsing both land and machinery as the most important asset leading to the accumulation of wealth. And data, it turns out, is much more difficult to regulate and own than land or machines. As best-selling author and historian Yuval Harari says, "Data are everywhere and nowhere at the same time, they can move at the speed of light, and you can create as many copies of them as you want."

When businesses operate by competing over resources—land, machinery, or information—they operate in more hierarchical and directive means. However, as data continues to be open-sourced, and as technology allows us to evolve into an increasingly connected and globalized society, the most successful companies are developing more egalitarian, collaborative, and bottom-up cultures. The ability to work well together is becoming more important than the ability to "win" a fight over resources.

Which is why, in this new era of business, companies must move forward by acknowledging our roots: we are, by nature, an altruistic species. It feels good to care for those around us. For the vast majority of the time our species has existed, we have been communal. Our intelligence is rooted in our social brains and in our ability to care for our individual and collective well-being by working together.

Chapter Ten

In the summer of 2018, the pregnant wife of a founder of a tech company asked me to help her convince her husband to take parental leave. At a recent panel where I'd spoken, she'd heard me talk about the many benefits of dads taking this time to be at home with their newborns. Soon after I started working with her, a handful of other pregnant women approached me to help them do the same with their tech founder husbands.

In coaching them, I first encouraged these women to tell their husbands about the positive impact it would have on them. Research has found that when a man takes leave, it significantly improves the long-term trajectory of their wives' careers. For instance, a 2010 Swedish study found mothers' future earnings increased 7% for every month of parental leave that her partner took. This, unfortunately, did not sway any of the men.

Next, I suggested that they tell their husbands about the many benefits it would have on their kids. When fathers take parental leave, they have been shown to be more involved in their kids' lives in future years. And according to research by Scott Coltrane from the University of Oregon, preschoolers with engaged fathers show higher levels of cognitive competence, self-control, and empathy. Researchers at Penn State have found that as adolescents, the children of actively caretaking dads have more self-esteem, especially the girls. This, also, did little to encourage their husbands to take time off.

Then, I worked with them to outline the many positive neurological changes a dad who takes responsibility for his newborn can experience. Earlier that year, after a session at Yelp where I'd discussed the many brain benefits a dad can earn by showing up for the first year of their child's life, a young male manager who was not yet a father came up to me and said: "I feel like I should immediately go out and have a kid so I can be better at my job." Armed with the same data I'd shared at Yelp, these women approached their husbands to explain how and why parental leave could benefit them. Again, we struck out. This information did not convince any of them.

The one thing that ultimately held some sway with a few of them was the financial bottom line. If they took leave, their wives explained, it would positively impact their ability to recruit and retain top talent inside the companies they had founded. It would send the message that their company was hospitable to people who wanted to tend to their lives outside of work, and this would make it a more desirable workplace. For instance, one study found that "83% of millennials would leave their job for one with better family/ lifestyle benefits." And, it would unlock many of the cultural norms that led to enhanced productivity—all of the skills outlined in earlier chapters of this book that lead to successful teams. I encouraged the wives to tell their husbands about Phil Farhi, the head of product for a tech company called Thumbtack. When one of Phil's male colleagues, who was also in the C-suite at his company, planned to come back to work right after his wife had given birth, Phil stopped him. "Look man," Phil told him, "that will send the wrong message to everyone here. It's really bad for company morale. You need to stay home."

Unfortunately, even this argument only convinced two of the founder dads to take any parental leave. And both of them hid their leave from the public eye— they explicitly counseled their communications teams to make sure that no one external to the company knew about their time away from work.

The rest of the dads did not take any real leave because—even though it might have a positive impact on their wives' careers, their child's development, their own brain's enhanced capacity to perform well, their current and prospective employees, and their overall company culture and its productivity—they feared it would have a long-term negative impact on their own professional reputation. "It would send a bad message to my investors," one man told his wife. "And I can't afford to jeopardize those relationships."

In working with these wives over several weeks and months, I discovered that these men weren't callous and disinterested. They genuinely wanted to be good dads and husbands; they wanted the best for their families. But they had a hard time seeing how this didn't all come down to the financial bottom line. Providing for their family's financial security, they believed, was their most important role as a father and husband. And taking leave, which all of them genuinely wanted to do, threatened their ability to be a good provider because our culture believes that taking the time to show up for parenthood means we aren't fully committed to our work.

At TendLab, we've been encouraging company leaders to set the tone from the top. To role model to their employees their own value of caretaking by taking parental leave and being actively engaged parents. But if even the founders of companies, when armed with all of the data around the benefits of leave, don't feel empowered to take leave, or to be public about it if they do, then where will the drive for systemic change for all parents come from?

To create the change we all need, we must work together to change our cultural narrative. Sharing facts isn't enough. We must shift our collective beliefs. Our communally-oriented great ancestors survived because they adhered to group norms and expectations. And we are still neurologically primed to act in alignment with those around us. "Our biology puts emphasis on social belonging as essential to survival, even over perceptual accuracy of the world," neuroscientist Michael Schmidt told me. "We are more likely to survive wrong but together than right and alone."

As a freshman in high school, I was selected to participate in a senior class psychology experiment. Sitting beside the three other fake "subjects" in front of a room full of seniors, I was asked to determine which two lines on a sheet of paper were similar in length. I was the last student to give my answer and I remember feeling disoriented as I looked at the black lines on the white paper. The room of older students waited for me, some snickering in the back, as I struggled to see what was right in front of me. Finally, I just blurted out the same answer everyone else had given. The room erupted in laughter. As someone escorted me out of the room, I crumpled the white sheet of paper into my coat pocket. Later that day, I took it out and smoothed it down on a table so I could get a good look at the lines. Away from the room of seniors, I could see that the answer I'd given was wrong.

This test was a variation of lab experiments first conducted in the 1950s. Back then, 75% of the time people made the same mistake as I did: they chose the wrong answer because everyone around them had said it was the right answer.

Gregory Berns, a professor of psychiatry at Emory University, recently decided to conduct a modified version of this same experiment while people were in brain scanners. He found that when everyone else chooses a false answer, the subject's brain goes wild. But here's the thing: the regions of the brain which light up are associated with processing visual information (the midbrain) and with experiencing fear (the amygdala). The part of our brain responsible for making conscious choices (prefrontal cortex) does not light up. We don't consciously choose to agree with those around us—our brain makes the decision for us. In other words, according to Berns, our brains are so wired to keep us within the confines of social norms that they change what we see.

Therefore, it's not enough to be presented with facts. We must change the social norms around parenthood and work. Fortunately, there are countries who have succeeded in doing this.

In the 1960s, a coalition of Nordic countries decided to create policies to make it easier for mothers to stay in the workforce. They found that while women with children did remain employed, they didn't rise into leadership positions; rather, they were "mommy-tracked" into jobs with no upward mobility. To design a solution that allowed women to progress in their careers, this coalition engaged in a multi-stakeholder approach, bringing together business leaders, politicians, celebrities, and others to collectively design a solution. Working together, they created family-friendly benefits that incentivized dads to engage in the early care of their children. In Sweden, for example, each family is granted a set amount of family leave—sixteen months—which can be shared between both parents. To inspire dads to take a portion of this leave, they've designated three months for the exclusive use of dads, or the "other" parent in non-heterosexual couples. This coalition also created a public awareness campaign: celebrity dads were seen with babies strapped to their fronts in cloth sacks, photos of muscular men with tattoos pushing babies in strollers were put up in car repair shops, and buses had murals of dads gathering together at bars with their infants in tow. This awareness campaign, coupled with the "use-it-or-lose-it" paternal leave policy, created a culture in which 90% of all fathers take at least three months of parental leave.

In just one generation, this coalition's actions have transformed cultural norms around caregiving in the Nordic countries. Sociologist Caitlin Collins has found that men in Sweden, whose fathers were not actively involved as caretakers in their own infancy, now consider taking this leave and caring for their young ones a "right," rather than a "duty." According to Collins, "the sense that fathers are entitled to time with their children helps normalize Swedish dads' participation in the child-rearing and absolves women of full responsibility for this caring labor." A Finnish friend of mine told me that in her workplace a man who doesn't take leave is considered 'defective.' Yeah," she told me, "everyone looks at the guy like there's something wrong with him."

Recent survey data indicates that the majority of Swedes—both men and women—believe parents should equally split parental leave, and the government has just begun to offer bonuses to couples who chose this 50:50 option. This impacts the workforce, because anyone could go out for parental leave—not just mothers. Women are no longer considered potential 'liabilities,' when men are just as likely to take a break from work to start their families. In fact, all women, not just mothers, fare better at work when men take parental leave: according to a recent joint study by the Peterson Institute for International Economics and EY of nearly 22,000 companies across ninety-one countries, all women are more likely to rise into leadership positions in countries where more men take parental leave.

The Nordic countries have shown us what is possible. We can transform our entire culture's perception of parenthood and work. We can reverse the stigma engaged parents are likely to face at work.

Katie Bethell, the founder of the advocacy organization PL+US, has been working hard to change the U.S.'s cultural norms around caretaking. Her ultimate goal is to pass legislation to provide federal funds for equal paid family leave for all. But instead of just lobbying in Washington, Katie focuses much of her time and attention on the business sector. Her study of other successful campaigns in the U.S., and her own experience, has shown her that "what business leaders want, the government will get behind. Not the other way around."

To influence business leaders, Katie and her team at PL+US have engaged in a multi-pronged approach:

they've worked inside companies, supporting and empowering internal employee advocates; they've done research and educated the media by sitting down with key journalists to share their findings; they've engaged with shareholder activists to support them in filing (or threatening to file) resolutions against companies who don't have paid leave, or who are discriminatory in their offerings; and they've engaged a strong base of supporters, including both donors and influential leaders.

Fortunately, parents inside companies have been organizing to advocate for themselves. A decade ago, there were virtually no parent Employee Resource Groups within companies. Today, there are hundreds of them. Lori Mihalich-Levin, who started the parenting Employee Resource Group at Dentons, the largest law firm in the world, began convening the leaders of parenting ERG's a few years ago. Today, her Working Parent Group Network includes 152 individuals representing 76 different organizations, in all different sectors—such as law, non-profit, CPGs, tech, fashion, accounting, government, and more—and they meet regularly to learn and share with each other. Back in February of 2017, I was at the first Parents in Tech Alliance (PTA) meeting, a secret gathering of parents leading the parents' groups inside the largest tech companies in the San Francisco Bay Area. That day, Sarah Johal, who had started the parenting group at Lyft, connected with someone on Katie's team at PL+US, who then worked closely with Sarah to help her launch a successful campaign at Lyft to win significantly expanded paid family leave for all parents, regardless of birth status.

Internal advocacy by employees is not always enough. "When the carrot doesn't work," Katie told me, "we use the stick." Determined to get paid family leave for everyone, not just employees on the higher end of the wage scale, PL+US has played a key role in getting several companies—such as Walmart, Starbucks, and CVS—to offer all levels of employees paid family leave. They've been successful because they've created a platform for parent employees to speak up for themselves; they've engaged the media in publicly shaming the companies who don't offer equal benefits to all classes of employees; and they've supported investors in filing shareholder resolutions stating that they are concerned about the risk of "employment discriminaton" that comes with not providing leave, or with only providing leave to high wage employees.

There are also leaders in the business community who are taking a public stand for parenthood. Alexis Ohanian, the founder of Reddit, took parental leave when his wife, Serena Williams, had their baby. In an <u>Op-Ed</u> for the New York Times he acknowledges that men who take leave are likely to be stigmatized. "But," he writes, "my message to these guys is simple: Taking leave pays off, and it's continued to pay dividends for me two years later. It should be no surprise that I also encourage all of our employees to take their full leave at Initialized Capital, where I am managing partner; we recently had three dads on paid paternity leave at the same time."

And there are others who are stepping up, too.

Chapter Eleven

One of the hardest things about running TendLab is believing in it. I am pushing so hard against our culture's conventional wisdom that I feel like the bird flying at the V-point at the front of the flock. The resistance I face, both within me and around me, is fierce.

I wake up every day much earlier than I would like to pack lunches and wipe noses and address tantrums. It is not glamorous or even enjoyable much of the time. The labor required to tend to little ones is often mundane, repetitive, and relentless. I am usually exhausted and frustrated by the time I finally get all three of my kids ready to start their days. I then spend the rest of my day either at my desk or inside an organization, explaining how and why caring for our kids—and each other—can make us better humans. I am sitting on mounds of research and interviews which clearly validate this hypothesis. The data is solid. But the daily grind of believing in it while operating in environments that do not recognize its truth is exhausting.

After learning about the social nature of our brains, and how we are wired for conformity, I decided that I needed to surround myself with other people who were working hard to claim the value of caregiving. In February of 2019, I formed a collaborative of other founders who are innovating around the needs of caregivers. When we met for the first time there were twenty-four of us—all women, almost all mothers or caregivers—seated around a conference table for a casual lunch. Almost everyone in the room had ventures more established and accomplished than TendLab. My friend Shadiah Sigala, the CEO and Co-founder of the child care platform Kinside, worked with me to bring the group together. In our email inviting the other founders, many of whom we'd never met before, we said we were hosting the gathering because we knew we were stronger together than we are alone. Together, we could play a role in shaping, driving, and naming the developing market for our businesses and services. Together, we could achieve greater individual success, and we could better elevate the mission we were all driving towards: increased support and value for caregivers. "A rising tide," we wrote, "lifts all boats."

Almost every woman we invited showed up.

One of the people in attendance was Patrice Martin, who at the time of this first gathering was working as an Entrepreneur in Residence at IDEO CoLab on a study of care in America with Pivotal Ventures, the incubation and investment company headed by Melinda Gates. Patrice and her team had spent an entire year interviewing families about the nature of caregiving in the United States. After interviewing families, she then went on to interview the founders of ventures designed to solve for the needs of caregivers. She found that many of the founders she spoke with had "an activist mindset," by which she meant they were, "committed to shaking up the status quo of unpaid labor and building businesses that actually get women and families the solutions they need to thrive."

The founders in the room were intimately familiar with the same headwind I was flying into every day. As women—and particularly as mothers—the statistical likelihood of us succeeding in acquiring funding for our ventures is abysmally low. In 2018, female founders received only 2.2% of all venture capital funding; and female founders of color received less than 1% of total funding.

Another problem we faced was that our ventures are designed to solve for the needs of caregivers. And even though the vast majority of Americans self-identify as caregivers, the investment industry still views this as a niche market with a limited potential for growth.

Lynn Perkins, the CEO of Urban Sitter, first sought venture funding back in 2011. The all-male venture capitalists she approached had had little exposure to the need for childcare. Lynn was even turned down by one firm because, of the two "niche" market ventures they were considering—Urban Sitter and a "luxury jet travel" start-up—they thought Lynn's business was the riskier proposition. Lynn proved them wrong and went on to raise over $40 million. She showed through her successful business, which is now operational in all fifty states, that the market for childcare is vast and growing.

It's still an uphill battle. Two years ago, Kate Torgersen, the Founder of Milk Stork, the first breast milk shipping company, was turned down by a prospective investor because, as he told her, "women who care about their careers are not going to breastfeed." And yet, Kate's business is succeeding: Milk Stork is offered as an employee benefit at over 600 companies and has doubled its revenue every year. At the time of writing, Milk Stork has delivered more than 2.6 million ounces of breastmilk.

Since our initial gathering, the group has met quarterly. When Shadiah moved to Los Angeles and could no longer invest time in the collaborative, Lynn Perkins stepped up to co-lead it with me. One of the most accomplished entrepreneurs in our group, Lynn's leadership has helped us grow. She regularly surveys our group, formally and informally, to get feedback and engagement from us. She facilitates highly-curated conversations during our gatherings which allow the group to delve into timely, critical issues. And perhaps most importantly, she serves as a powerful role model for the types of engagements we aim to foster. She's spent years constructively engaging with other founders in the space—even her direct competitors—because she knows it's good, not only for her business, but for the overall market. Lynn's candor and transparency also sets the tone for our community; when she openly talks about the challenges she faces, it creates the space for others to do the same. Erin Beck—a former rocket scientist for SpaceX and a spacecraft operator for NASA who left her career in science to launch a collaborative childcare platform called The Wana Family Network—stepped up to actively manage our Slack channel. Erin continues to cultivate our highly engaged online community by creating focused channels, leading conversations generous in asks and gives, and inviting other founders into our community.

We collectively decided to expand the group to include founders of all genders. And people started flying in from other states to join our gatherings.

At the end of 2019, one of Kate Torgersen's investors, a woman named Courtney Leimkuhler, reached out to me. She and two partners were launching an investment firm venture called the Springbank Collective. Their thesis was that the "gender gap" was in large part a function of the massive gap in infrastructure to support women and working families. They were investing in young companies that were building that missing infrastructure for both work and home. They weren't a typical venture capital fund; they wanted to build an ecosystem of investors, employers, social sector advocates for women and families, and entrepreneurs to tackle these problems in a holistic way. And they had a hunch based on what they had seen through Kate's involvement with the San Francisco group, that there would be significant business and personal benefit to founders in the emerging care sector from collaborating with each other. When they asked for my advice, I suggested they support me in building out our San Francisco-based community to a national scale. And they did, joining Lynn and me as co-founders of what soon became a national-in-scope community of founders solving for the needs of caregivers.

Together with Courtney Leimkuhler from Springbank, I spent the early part of 2020 traveling the country meeting with groups of founders innovating around caregiving. I discovered that almost every founder was not just passionate about the success of their own venture, but also about creating better conditions for caregivers. The market for our services was nascent, but rapidly growing. No one had a venture that had existed for longer than ten years; and the majority of them had launched after I'd started TendLab in 2016. I was amazed to discover that there were so many of us committed to creating better conditions for caregivers

Almost every founder I spoke with had a deeply personal story behind their business. Melissa Hanna at Mahmee, a virtual maternity and pediatric care coordination platform, had watched her mother, an award-winning nurse and international board certified lactation consultant, work tirelessly for decades to design maternity and breastfeeding programs for top- tier hospitals and health systems that consistently lacked the essential technologies required to stay connected with high-risk mothers and newborns once they were discharged. As she told me, "Maternal healthcare in the United States is more expensive than it is in almost any other country, but in this case, price is not a signal of quality. It can cost as much as ten times more to have a baby in the United States, and yet we have the highest maternal mortality rate of all industrialized nations. How is it that we spend the most and get the worst results in return?" Jason Lehmbeck had a harrowing time trying to get his son with multiple disabilities accurately diagnosed and treated, so he launched Team Special X to help parents of special needs children navigate their journeys with greater ease. Allyson Downey, the founder of WeeSpring & Stellar Reviews, had faced severe pregnancy discrimination when she was at Credit Suisse; Debi Yadegari of MommaWork was told if she became pregnant, she would be ruining her career by a female superior—within the legal department no less!—when she worked at Lehman Brothers. Lindsay Jurist-Rosner, founder of Wellthy, was her mother's caregiver for twenty-eight years as she fought a decades-long battle with primary progressive Multiple Sclerosis. Lindsay said this experience was extremely challenging for her as a young professional, because she felt she had to hide her extensive caretaking responsibilities to avoid losing her professional credibility. Lindsay started Wellthy to ease the burden for other working families as they care for aging, chronically ill, or disabled loved ones.

And the founders in our space were finding their way to incubators like TechStars and Y-combinator. They were cobbling together resources—from their own personal savings, from friends and family rounds, and even, in some cases, from VCs—to get their ventures off the ground. And while we were finding our way, most of us were working in isolation, not meaningfully connected to others who were also pushing hard to develop viable businesses and to claim the value and relevance of our work. Our mental health was constantly challenged. As Jessica Chang at WeeCare told us, "I've founded and run successful ventures before. But this is my first time running a business with a deeply personal mission. And it takes a much greater toll on me, because I care about it so much."

When the COVID-19 pandemic struck, our group mobilized almost overnight to provide resources and support for families. Mary Beth Ferrante, a member of our collaborative and the founder of WRK/360, wrote an article about our collaborative for *Forbes*. In the piece, she cites how twenty-seven of our founders came together to create a safety net for caregivers. Collectively, we produced guides and resources for caregivers and their employers; offered free online classes and complimentary home cooking kits for kids; gave no-cost babysitting to essential workers; provided free access and free onboarding assistance to maternal and infant care providers who needed to quickly transition their in-office and in-home care to a virtual format; collected and shared advice about how parents of children with special needs could cope with a pause in therapeutic services; and pushed hard for legislation, such as the Families First Coronavirus Response Act, to create federal support for caregivers.

Today, our collaborative is national in scope and includes more than 120 founders of ventures ranging from seed stage to Series D. Collectively, we've raised over $1 billion dollars. And we continue to grow, as any member is welcome to invite another founder into our community.

As a group, we are committed to deepening the connections within our community, and expanding to include new members, so we can bring visibility to the rapidly growing industry that is fam tech. And we are dedicated to doing this while actively working to dismantle gender stereotypes; fostering an economy of caregivers with visibility, voice and value; pursuing diversity and equity at all organizational levels; and creating jobs with dignity.

We are hopeful that we are at a tipping point, that the needs of caregivers are finally becoming visible and valid, and that resources and other critical forms of support we need will be more readily available for our ventures.

And our group is collaborating: going to market with bundled services, joining each other's advisory boards, sharing staff, developing revenue shares, engaging in joint marketing campaigns, and more.

Every day our Slack channel lights up with questions, requests, celebrations, and pictures of our loved ones—the kids, elders, and friends we are caring for—as well as with encouragement. On a recent afternoon when I was struggling, Erin Beck sent me a private message,

"You make the world look beautiful, just like you!"

This peer support and engagement—from others who are forging themselves through similar challenges for the same cause—matters.

Conclusion

As a culture, we are at a crossroads. Humankind has never before faced such rapid change. Our current pandemic, economic globalization, the drastic changes to our natural environment, including climate change, and the rapid pace of technological development are all forcing us to reckon with our current ways of being in relationship to ourselves and to the world.

We've been taught that we must act independently. That to succeed is to forsake our connections—with ourselves and with the people around us. This is false.

Our fates are bound up with one another. We all have a part to play in the story of our time. Now, more than ever before, we must recognize and value that which makes us uniquely human: our social brains. By nature, we are both collective and altruistic.

Parenthood, possibly more than anything else, enhances the social quality of our brains. It's time for us to recognize that the skills developed while parenting—such as adaptability and resilience, and the ability to have deeper, more authentic relationships with one another—are the skills we all need to develop, regardless of whether we ever have kids. And it's time for all of us to take a stand for the value of the experiences that allow us to develop these skills. We must invest in the well-being of our workplaces by implementing policies to support all caregivers; and incentivizing all employees, regardless of their gender, caregiver status, or income level, to value the power of vulnerability, empathy, and collaboration. We also need federal legislation—such as paid family leave for all, and subsidized early childhood education—which acknowledges that the greatest reflection of our culture is how we care for our parents and caregivers.

At the time that I am writing this conclusion, it's been eight months since the World Health Organization announced that COVID was a global pandemic. And almost every working parent I know is overwhelmed with the stress of parenting during COVID. We are grappling with too many things—tending to and educating our children while maintaining our careers—while also reckoning with the implications of a world that is in flux.

Many parents are opting out of the workforce because they can't handle it. In September alone, 865,000 <u>women</u>, almost all mothers, quit their jobs. Other recent reports have indicated that up to 54% of working parents are considering leaving their jobs if they are unable to find regular child care. Many of us were stressed and under-resourced before the pandemic struck, and now we are visibly buckling under the weight of too much responsibility.

I wrote this book to share with you, and to reinforce within myself, the path forward. This moment is an opportunity for transformation. In the face of our culture's inaccurate perception of parenthood's impact on career performance, we can choose to see—and act—in alignment with the truth. We can recognize that showing up for parenthood gives us the opportunity to evolve into more potent versions of our former selves; and we can take advantage of this opportunity by doing the deep work necessary to change—not just ourselves, but the world around us, too.

Pierre Omidyar's Hope Lab has spent decades exploring why some people encounter trauma and are able to grow through the experience, becoming wiser and more compassionate and effective, while others never fully recover and remain shells of their former selves. They've found that people who are resilient in the wake of trauma have three things in common: a sense of connection with others; a sense of agency; and a sense of purpose.

Learning about this research helped me understand the healing journey I've been on for the past twenty years. Prior to becoming a mother, my ability to be an effective agent of change was limited because I didn't think others could see or understand me. No matter where I went, I felt like an outsider. But after becoming a mom, I recognized that I was a part of a continuum of life that extended deep into the past and far into the future, and—whether I liked it or not—I belonged and was essential. As my friend Pat Callair, a grandmother and civil rights activist who trained with Martin Luther King, Jr. told me, "Once you become a parent, your life is no longer just your own." The daily surrender to the tending of my kids connects me to others who are doing the same thing. Mothers and fathers all over the world, and throughout all of time, wake up late at night to feed and soothe babies and quell toddler's night terrors, and then they go to work in the mornings tired and bleary eyed, with unkempt hair and spit up on their shirts. None of us are alone in these experiences. But in the U.S., we often feel like we are. When I reached out to my mom friends, and then to their friends and to dads and parents of all genders, I discovered that we were all experiencing similar versions of the exact same thing. And when I tapped into the pulse of energy that came from being in relationship to those who could both see and understand me—and who were aware of their humble place within a greater continuum of life—something in me healed. We need to know that we are not alone. When we tap into this awareness, we access our capacity to evolve.

There are many things over which we have no control. We cannot bring back the lives that have been—and will continue to be—lost to the virus. We cannot speed up the clinical trials creating the vaccines. We cannot stop the tornadoes hitting the East Coast with increasing ferocity or the wildfires that cripple California every year. But we can look at the places within us in need of tending. With great care, we can touch the old wounds that are surfacing and trace them back to their roots. If we give them the space they need to be acknowledged and felt, they will heal. And after we have sat with the terror of our own dissolution in the face of pain or trauma that once felt too great to bear, we become less reactive, less defensive, and less afraid. And when we emerge from the fortresses that once protected us from the things we feared, we put down the old things which no longer serve us. We ask ourselves: "Does this habit, activity, or relationship make me feel more alive?" If the answer is "No," then we use whatever agency we have to make a better choice.

After some time, this deep internal work frees us up to become a part of a bigger solution. And not just for our own lives, but for all of us. When we step into this momentum and energy, we experience a quickening. I promise you, there is a tide swelling. And you are needed inside it's roiling rise. Each one of us has a specific role to play in the creation of a better future. And we will know our place when we feel lit up—from the inside—with joy and purpose.

Going deeper in the creation of this book was my action in response to the panic that threatened to overwhelm me when COVID struck. Putting pen to paper and words to screen gave me the opportunity to integrate all of the experiences I've had in the last twenty years. The most important thing I've learned is that relationships matter: my relationship to myself, and to the tender places within me; my relationships with my family, friends, colleagues, and greater community; and my relationship to our culture.

While I illuminate moments of sorrow and suffering in this narrative, the experience ultimately proved redemptive in a way that makes my entire body vibrate with a blissful, "Yes." My hands feel electric as I move them across my keyboard, my bare feet tap on the carpet with the rhythm that moves these words through me, and my breath flows deep and full into my chest and belly.

I hope you hear the resonance of the message I've poured into these pages. I hope something I've shared has touched a tender place within you in need of companionship. I hope you know you are not alone and I hope you feel called to action. You are part of a much bigger story that needs you.

Acknowledgments

Writing a book has been a lifelong dream. As a little girl, I imagined it would be a solitary endeavor: I would shut myself away for months or years and emerge with a masterpiece untouched by anyone else. And while there are some parts of this book that I crafted in isolation the vast majority of this book was a co-creative process. *Tending* is the culmination of over five years of conversations, interviews, and in-depth engagements with my family, other parents, researchers, founders, companies, and organizations.

Tending uses my own story as a starting point, as the flashlight I wield to look into the lives, stories, and research of hundreds of others. In this book, I attempt to make visible an aspect of our lives that has been in the shadows for far too long.

I am deeply grateful to the 228 parents who generously and courageously shared their stories with me. I promised to maintain the confidentiality of everyone I interviewed, but you know who you are. THANK YOU! I hope this book honors your experiences.

The researchers and other experts who've spent their careers exploring the future of humanity—as it relates to parenthood, and so much more—also played an invaluable role in the creation of this book.

Two researchers, in particular, showed me science's power to dismantle bias and oppression. Evolutionary anthropologist Sarah Blaffer Hrdy welcomed me into her home, spent many hours sharing her research and personal story with me, and read and commented on the entire first draft of this book. Her profound discoveries liberated me from the shaming belief that I was the only one capable of giving my kids all they need. Neuroscientist Ruth Feldman's research into the parental brain further underscored this, as she discovered that a dad's brain may be able to experience changes as drastic as a biological breastfeeding birth mother. I've listened to the interview I recorded with her more times than I can count.

Victoria Dimitrakopoulos of Project Brain Heart is responsible for my understanding that our human genius, that which separates us from all other primates and advanced species, is our social brain. She taught me this by sharing the science behind this insight; and in graciously allowing me to "share" her brain in crafting this book, particularly Chapter Three. Alexandra Sacks continues to be a beacon for me and for all mothers as she works to lift the veil of silence that would keep us mired in shame. I am grateful to you, Ali, for the many conversations we've shared, both on stage and off. Neuroscientist Michael Schmidt—who read this book as a father, a scientist, and a community builder—improved this book with his hard-earned wisdom. Heather Ainsworth's decades worth of experience advocating on behalf of caregivers in the workplace shaped the creation of this book. I'm also grateful to

Katherine Goldstein, Eve Rodsky, Sarah Lacy, Christine Michael Carter, Sara Mauskopf, Jill Koziol, Mary Beth Ferrante, and Blessing Adeysian for your leadership around improving our relationship to motherhood, and parenthood more broadly. And Tina Lee, I see you, friend! I know how much you've done for us all. Some of the other researchers and thought leaders whose work heavily influenced me are: Anne-Marie Slaughter, Brigid Schulte, Joan Williams, Josh Levs, and Shelley Correll.

I would also like to acknowledge the parents who are advocating for other parents from inside their companies, and the people who are supporting them in making this possible: Jaclyn Fitch and Floren Robinson for breaking ground at Accenture; Cristina Tcheyan for her courage and passion, and for publishing her "Why I'm Quitting Google" letter, which outlines the changes corporate America could make to more meaningfully support her and other parents; Eliza Kuzner, for her similar advocacy on behalf of parents at Facebook; Vanessa Loder and Liz Devlin for starting the Parents in Tech Alliance, and Amel Zahid who runs this group; Sarah Johal, who won a significantly expanded paid leave for all parents at Lyft and started Workday's parent ERG; Henri Loh, who leads through listening and has created the conditions necessary for the C-suite at Airbnb to do the same; Matt Burke for his courage in writing about his experience with his wife's postpartum depression and for his commitment to leading by example; Jenny Snyder for continuing to show up, even in the face of significant resistance; Alison Crawford, a formidable parent advocate at Uber; Adam Rhuberg, whose infographic of how he spent his time on paternity leave is framed on my wall; and Lori Mihalich-Levin for her leadership, as she started Denton's parents' group and has been connecting and convening all of the parents' leading the parents' groups at their companies across the country; and the rest of Katie Bethell's team at PL+US, such as Orli Cortel and Annie Sartor, for their powerful support of parent-advocates and their incredible work advocating for federal policy change.

Janet Van Huysse, my co-founder at TendLab, who is the most glamorous woman I know and who is beloved by all who work with her. Thanks, Janet, for taking the leap with me. Jim Van Huysse, for his commitment to living with heart. Kim (Weisberg) Rohrer, our newest co-founder and COO at TendLab, I'm so grateful to be in your enormous fan club and thrilled to be partnering with you, too: here's to putting relationships first, and to having a big impact together. Katrine Strickland, I am grateful for your calm, level-headed passion. I hope we will be working together for a long time to come.

To all of the people who played a valuable role in the development of TendLab: Dina Kwan, Sara Roos-Essl, Nathalie Miller, Sonya Zilka, Erica Priggen-Wright, Hugh Molotsi, Danielle Vallurupalli, Erin Faverty,

Mary Beth Ferrante, Marisa Lopez, Aimee Cubbage, Patrice Martin, Shadiah Sigala, Maya & Matt Markovich, Abigail Sommerfeld, Stacey Delo, Alexandra Sacks M.D., Adele Burnes, Anne Shaw, Chetna Seghal, Ashley Abramson, Jo Piazza, Lanya Zambrano, Ellen Heirbaut, Cheryl Contee, Merritt Quisumbing, Kate Reading, Robbie Peters, Anne Shaw, and Kate Torgersen.

Thank you to all of the founders in our Fam Tech collaborative—you've all launched ventures designed to solve for the needs of caregivers and you're also showing up to play your part in advocating for larger, systemic change. Lynn Perkins,' the way you've volunteered to lead this collaborative with me—even while serving as the CEO of your own sizable company in the midst of a global pandemic with drastic fluctuations in your business and all of your kids at home and needing your care—is a testament to your generosity of spirit! The opportunity to partner with you in this work has been one of the greatest blessings in this decade of my life. Courtney Leimkuhler, your presence has catalyzed much growth, both within our collaborative and in me, and I am grateful to you for your willingness to show up for all of the hard, necessary conversations and for your genuine commitment to change. The other Springbank Collective partners, Elana Berkowitz and Jen Lee Koss, have also been powerful allies. Erin Beck, our late-night video chats with Fae in the background are some of my favorite memories from this past year; your passion for life inspires me. Shadiah

Sigala, thanks for recognizing that this group needed to come together; I'll never forget the conversation about our grandmothers that fueled our enthusiasm for its creation. Jessica Rolph, who has been a source of support in some key moments, and whose previous work, partnering with Lara Jackle Dickinson to launch the Climate Collaborative, inspired my vision for our community. Christine Michel Carter, your passion and ability to mobilize others has been a gift. Adrienne Prentice and Rachel Johnson-Farias, for meeting with me for weeks to help determine the best legal status for our group. Nikki Adamson, for her inclusive heart and willingness to take over the membership process. Leslie Borrell, for showing us how to partner and leading the way. Felicia Kasheroff, for deepening our relationships to one another by ushering us through and into smaller peer groups. Charlotte Michalidis, for taking over Slack and supporting and incubating dreamers with ideas on the [can't read note here]. Cristina Tcheyan, for our late-night conversations that fed my soul and your ability to recruit great folks into our group. To Elizabeth Clubb, who could teach Diane Sawyer how to interview people, and Lynn Perkins, for hosting the best-ever pre-launch party. And to Eve Rodsky, Sarah Lacy, Blessing Adesiyan, Leslie Forde, Purva Gujar, and Kate Torgersen, for your kind words. And to all of the other founders volunteering to build, support, and expand our community—such as, Ari Rozman, Cait Zogby, Jen Saxton, Jessica Chang, Ann Crady-Weiss,

Joanna McFarland, Samantha Barnes, SJ Sacchetti, Priya Amin, Felicia Kasheroff, Kristin Langenfeld, Dirk Doebler, Matt Glickman, Ilnort Rueda, Pedro Silva, Samantha Rudolph, Arielle McKenzie, Jessica Toh, Evan Leaphart, Melissa Hanna, Sascha Mayer, Michael Walsh, Jessica Gupta, Arianna Taboada, Lindsay Jurist-Rosner, Sapna Saptagopan.

Readers who heavily influenced this book include Ami Hamilton, whose intuition is uncannily wonderful; Eliza Kuzner, for her courage and vulnerability; and Gabriela Beran, a kindred spirit who is also working to identify the career-relevant skills motherhood develops.

To my beloved editors Jane Anne Staw, thank you for continuing to 'see' me when I can't find myself, your kindness heals; Rae Abileah, whose activist heart makes better things possible; Sophie Lewis, whose wisdom far exceeds her age, and whom I look forward to following someday; Mikel Inchausti, your passion for justice and your love of footnotes has earned you a forever place in my heart; and Jesse Coleman, who has encouraged me from the beginning, and who is capable of expressing so much in a only few words, the mark of one who truly understands the craft of writing.

Jeanine Saperstein, for creating a community of 'Butterfly Moms," and for ushering us along our journeys with generosity and grace. To the women in this community who have inspired and supported me: Anya Emerson, Lara Jackle Dickinson, Sunny Saperstein, Kate Hamilton, Laetitia Mailhes, Sharon Teresa Louisell, Elizabeth Echols, Hilary Mitchell, Deborah Trivisonno, Amy Tobin, Tierra Forte, and Delilah Sarabia.

To the power couple committed to unearthing the stories of our modern time—Jay and Ahri Golden: We've been walking beside each other for many years and it's wonderful to be in partnership with you right now. Leah Lamb, for being my forever sister in this journey of using story as medicine. To Erica Priggen, for her deep intuition around design and branding. To Sorcha Rochford, for midwifing me through the process of using software as an organizing tool. To the team at Techtonica, especially Mar and Ned, for showing me how being an outsider prepared me to build a movement. To Dot Fisher-Smith, for modeling compassionate action and living with a fierce commitment to joy.

To the "Faithful Virgins" Stephanie Hess, my fellow home-town girl who made her dreams come true; Lucy Farey-Jones, who offered me wings when I needed them most; and Cheryl Porro, who shows me what flight looks like.

My incredible community of friends and loved ones—Sara and John Canepa, Lana Nguyen, Seana Condit-Gordon, Melissa Diaz, Jess and Carl Desimas, Alison Giltrap, Heidi Gibson, Jessica Fehringer, Lana Nguyen, Jennifer Makohka, Asia Plahar, Dallas and Chris Constantino, Paula Pagniez, Tayari Jones, Lynne Cox, Betty Wilhout, Jane Burton, Patrick McDonnell and Susan O'Connell, Patricia Latimer, Matt Kinoshita, T-M Baird, Naomi Epel, Mayah Curtis, Amy Benziger,

Amy Bibeau, Amy Cheney, Ragnar Borenson, Heidi Haavik, Mariana Hernandez, Lindsay Albrecht, Jennie Coleman, Micki Corti, Sarah Dorsey, Miakoda, Abby Miller & Alex Gudich, Rebecca Newburn, Rebecca Trobe, Kate Seely, Romy Peloquin, Karla Reiss, Emmy Rhine, Holly Roberson, and Jen Kim—who helped to plant and nourish the seeds within me that would become this book.

Antonia Jackson, who I named my second "mom" when I was seventeen after she reluctantly opened her dorm room door to me, and whose wise presence along with her parents, Calvin and Ethel Mae Jackson, changed the trajectory of my life. To the family Toni and I built together: Gino Pastori-Ng, Amanda Greene, Jocelyn Corbett, and all the mentors and youth who worked with us. We learned so much together. Aris Alhino and Brad Saums, who show up with tools— hammers, nails, empanadas, wisdom, and so much more—when I am most in need of renovations.

To the mentors, guides, healers, and teachers in my life—Pat Callair, Jacqueline Jennings, Rosa Gonzalez, Lisa Hwang, Cristina Pacheco, Dena Trujillo, Bob Richter, Joon Ho Shin, Gwen Jones, Nancy Newport, Lynn Sydney, David Hytha, Jeanette Swearengen, Vidar Jorgensen, Laurel Parnell, Brian Delate, Mary Anderson, Harley Harris, Paula McGuire, Genesa Greening, Kalimah Priforce, Ayori Selassie, Jo Townsen, Cynthia Chandler, Shannon Bevers, Kim Foster, and Brian Delate.

To the "allo-parents" in my kids' lives. Their god-parents—Clint Henderson, Lanette Otvos, Rachel Kaufman, JT Henderson, Jess Downs, Chris and Dayane Scott, and Nikki Silvestri—whose investment in Clare, Aidan, and Grace make them infinitely better humans. Clint, ever since you gave Clare her first Barbie—which I swore she'd never have!—before she was even born, you've been a generous presence in their lives. Lanette, my BFF since the first day of high school, your steady presence has meant so much to us all. Rachel, you have made their birthday parties, and fifth birthdays, and brought order and beauty into our new home—you are an integral part of our lives. JT, for the tenderness you bring. Jess Downs, for sharing your love of life. Nikki Silvestri, for letting Grace climb on your hair and for honoring the shadows. Dayane Alcanfor Scott, for loving them as your own—which they are!. For my brother Chris Scott, who sees and feels more than he can express in words, and who I'm proud to call my "kid" brother.

All of the other relatives and chosen family who play a part in raising Clare, Aidan, and Grace: Wallace Wortman, my ninety-seven year-old grandfather, whose passion for life inspires us all; Mary Kay Kennedy, "Mimi," for her loving and generous and ever-present support; Mike Remer, the funniest man I know who also has a huge heart; Tom Henderson, for giving them a home in one of the toughest, kindest places on earth; Lisa Bracero and Rosie Anderson for their open hearts;

Alicia, Matt, and JoyLynn for welcoming us into the family; Mary and Tom Wortman, for their tender care; Nancy Wortman, for the incredibly thoughtful holiday cards and gifts; Lewis Semprini, for sharing your love of nature on butterfly walks; Julia Semprini, for sharing your love of art; Madelyn Burger, Andrew Hippert, and baby Etta Rose for all the joy you inspire; Andrew Burger, for *not* modeling his two-year-old behavior (attacking me with kisses) around my children; Marilyn, Jason, and Johnny Camp and Jennifer and Fermin Lau, for the holidays of merriment and joy; Peggy, Bob, and Shelby Oxenford, for the generous gifts and humor; the Kennedy clan—Ann, Lisa, and Mark Langley, Emily Costello, Katie and Pete Huges, Theresa Willard, Jennifer Knowles and Kyle and James Hughes, Doug Kennedy and Scott Romelin, for their good-natured, warm hearts; Barbara and Sara Nabors, being in your presence feels like sitting in the center of my heart; Molly Flanagan, for the nature walks and the bird-tending kit, and for being our coach for the important things; Mart Bailey and Kila Remiker for all the love, support, wisdom, and delicious meals; Lyn, Emily, Terry, and Carol Clapham, for their open arms, generous hearts, and laughter; Tori Lewis, for "Butthead" and "Whale Shit," and for being my favorite writing companion, comedian, and home furnisher; for all the other Lewises—Sophie, Mina, Nico, and Jason—for being a sanctuary for us. To Molly Andrus, for teaching us how planting seeds with joy leads to beauty, both in a garden and in a person. And we love Izzy Andrus, too!

To the other teachers in my childrens' lives: Sharon Kovalevsky, your energy and passion mean everything; Brian Senf, for inspiring Aidan to love learning; Roberta Hunter, for inspiring Clare to believe in herself; Kara Scanlon, for your generous heart and open zoom room; the Woodroe Woods teachers especially Kathy, Joanne, Diane, Valerie, and Martha.

To the three women I gathered with while gestating this book: Nikki Silvestri, who brought us all together and whose bright spirit continues to impact us; Laura Harris, who welcomes me into myself with her breathtakingly kind sight; and Lea Endres, who believes in the power of story to connect us to ourselves, to each other, and to a better future. Thank you, Lea, for being my companion in the *Here We Are* conversation that was the genesis for this book; thank you Laura for putting the best versions of us onto the screen in this film. Lea, I am also beyond grateful to you for your understanding of how story, community, and technology are the forces that must come together if we wish to create change today. Thank you for both investing in me and partnering with me to wield these powerful tools on behalf of caregivers here in the U.S.

To the man who raised me as his daughter, Dennis Scott: I am in awe of your work ethic and your ability to keep your heart open.

To Shane, the father of my children: it has not been an easy road, and we are not where we thought we'd be;

but I am grateful for your presence in my life. We grew up together in more ways than one, and I hope this next phase of our lives brings us both much happiness.

Finally, to my children. Clare, may you continue to believe in yourself, even when no one else does. Just like the shattered glass candle holder you put back together in Montana, which none of us thought could be fixed, you have a gift for mending things, including the people you love. Aidan, your wise heart gives me hope for the future, and your tenderness is everything. When you were five, you were convinced that you and your wife would wake up in the middle of the night, get in your car, and drive to my house to get in my bed and snuggle with me. Grace, you know yourself better than anyone I've ever met. Just like when you were four and you got your coat and your purse and headed over to Zayn's birthday party by yourself, you have a clear vision of what you want and how to go about getting it. I am in awe of the light that shines through you.

Notes

Chapter One

14   *In a few years:* Feldman, Ruth. "The adaptive human parental brain: implications for children's social development." Trends in neurosciences vol. 38,6 (2015), pp. 387-99. pubmed.ncbi.nlm.nih.gov/25956962/.

14   *And I would also:* Rima, Brandi N, et al. "Reproductive Experience and the Response of Female Sprague-Dawley Rats to Fear and Stress." Comparative Medicine vol 59(5), Oct. 2009, pp. 437-443, ncbi.nlm.nih.gov/pmc/articles/PMC2771599/.

15   *These changes lasted a lifetime:* Kinsley, Craig H, et al. "Motherhood and Hormones of Pregnancy Modify Concentrations of Hippocampal Neuronal Dendritic Spines." PubMed, 17 May 2005.

15   *And as he told:* "Science agrees: Moms courageous, cool." CNN, 28 Oct. 2003, cnn.com/2003/HEALTH/parenting/10/28/motherhood.stress.reut/index.html.

Chapter Three

34   *In sociologist Caitlyn Collins':* Collins, Caitlyn. Making Motherhood Work. Princeton, Princeton University Press, 2019, pp. 1-26.

35   *This means that:* "NCS: Employee Benefits in the U.S., March 2014." Bureau of Labor Statistics, US Government, 2014, bls.gov/ncs/ebs/benefits/2014/ownership/civilian/table32a.pdf.

35   *In the U.S.,:* Malik, Rasheed, et al. "America's Childcare Deserts in 2018." Center for American Progress, 6 Dec. 2018, americanprogress.org/issues/early-childhood/reports/2018/12/06/461643/americas-child-care-deserts-2018/.

35   "Employment Characteristics of Families Summary." U.S. Bureau of Labor Statistics, U.S. Bureau of Labor Statistics, 21 Apr. 2020, bls.gov/news.release/famee.nr0.htm.

35   *Working Mothers today:* "Chapter 4: How Mothers and Fathers Spend Their Time." Pew Research Center's Social & Demographic Trends Project, 31 Dec. 2019, pewsocialtrends.org/2013/03/14/chapter-4-how-mothers-and-fathers-spend-their-time/.

35   *This is especially true:* Bianchi, Suzanne, et al. "Maternal Employment and Family Caregiving: Rethinking Time with Children in the ATUS." Department of Sociology and Maryland Population Research Center (MPRC) University of Maryland, 9 Dec. 2005, atususers.umd.edu/papers/atusconference/authors/Bianchi.pdf.

36   *And third, according:* Williams, Joan, et al. What Works for Women at Work: Four Patterns Working Women Need to Know. New York University Press, 2018.

36   *In 2007, Shelley:* Correll, Shelley J., et al. "Getting a Job: Is There a Motherhood Penalty?" American Journal of Sociology, vol. 112, no. 5, Mar. 2007, pp. 1297-1339, sociology.stanford.edu/sites/g/files/sbiybj9501/f/publications/getting_a_job-_is_there_a_motherhood_penalty.pdf.

36   *And it may be:* Oster, Emily. "End the Plague of Secret Parenting." The Atlantic, Atlantic Media Company, 14 June 2019, the atlantic.com/ideas/archive/2019/05/normalize-parenthood-workplace-dont-hide-it/589822/.

36   *The United States has one:* Kleven, Henrik, et al. "Children and Gender Inequality: Evidence from Denmark." NBER Working Paper Series, Jan. 2018, henrikkleven.com/uploads/3/7/3/1/37310663/kleven-landais-sogaard_nber-w24219_jan2018.pdf. (says to include copyright notice)

36   *For all of these reasons:* "Pg. 98." Lean In, by Sheryl Sandberg, Random House UK, 2015.

36   *They encounter greater discrimination:* Thomas, Rachel, et al. "Women in the Workplace 2019." McKinsey & Company, 2019, wiwreport.s3.amazonaws.com/Women_in_the_Workplace_2019.pdf

    Chapter Four

44   *Evolutionary anthropologist Sarah Hrdy is widely:* "The Evolution of Motherhood." PBS, 25 Oct. 2009, pbs.org/wgbh/nova/article/evolution-motherhood/.

44   *Sarah's main mentor:* Magurran, Anne. "Maternal Instinct." The New York Times, 23 Jan. 2000. nytimes.com/2000/01/23/books/maternal-instinct.html

45   *Rather, "they are inseparably:* Ellison, Katherine. The Mommy Brain: How Motherhood Makes Us Smarter. New York, Basic Books, 2005, pp. 115.

46   *Third, infants cared for by:* Hrdy, Sarah Blaffer. Mothers and Others: The Evolutionary Origins of Mutual Understanding. Cambridge, the Belknap Press, 2009.

47   *Relative to other primates:* Max Planck Institute studies: Rubin, John, director. Ape Genius. PBS, NOVA - National Geographic Special, 0AD, pbs.org/wgbh/nova/video/ape-genius/. Accessed 4 July 2020.

Chapter Five

54   *The daughter of a:* Dickey, Megan Rose. "The 25 Most Influential African-Americans In Technology." Business Insider, 4 Apr. 2013, businessinsider.com.au/most-influential-blacks-in-technology-2013-4#2-shellye-archambeau-24.

57   *Feldman's research indicates:* Saturn, Sarina R. "Flexibility of father's brain." Proceedings of the National Academy of Sciences of the United States of America, vol. 111(27), 8 Jul. 2014, pp. 4671- 4672. pnas.org/content/111/27/9671.full.

60   *Recently, Feldman published:* Feldman, Ruth. "The adaptive human parental brain: implications for children's social development." Trends in neurosciences vol. 38,6 (2015), pp. 387-99. pubmed.ncbi.nlm.nih.gov/25956962/.

65   *And even when:* Green, Jeff. "Dads Say They Deserve Parental Leave But Only in Theory."Bloomberg, 18 Apr. 2018, bloomberg.com/news/articles/2018-04-18/dads-say-they-deserve-parental-leave-even-if-they-don-t-take-it.

65   *Michelle Budig, a:* Budig, Michelle J. "The Fatherhood Bonus and The Motherhood Penalty: Parenthood and the Gender Gap in Pay." Third Way, 2 Sept. 2014. thirdway.org/report/the-fatherhood-bonus-and-the-motherhood-penalty-parenthood-and-the-gender-gap-in-pay.

65   *If they do:* Berdahl, Jennifer L., Sue H. Moon. "Workplace Mistreatment of Middle Class Workers Based on Sex, Parenthood, and Caregiving." Journal of Social Issues vol. 69(2), 2013, pp. 341-366. -2.rotman.utoronto.ca/facbios/file/Berdahl%20&%20Moon.pdf.

66   *Mary Beth Ferrante:* "Training and development platform for working parents." WRK360, wrk360.com/.

67   *Derek Rotondo filed:* "EEOC Charge - Derek Rotondo." ACLU, aclu.org/legal-document/eeoc-charge-derek-rotondo.

67   *"I think all…":* Schmidt, Samantha. "JPMorgan Chase settles class-action lawsuit after dad demands equal parental leave for men." The Washington Post, 30 May 2019, washingtonpost.com/dc-md-va/2019/05/30/dads-win-settlement-with-jpmorgan-chase-over-parental-leave-policy/.

68   *Recent research out of:* Feldman, Ruth, et al. "The Human Coparental Bond Implicates Distinct Corticostriatal Pathways: Longitudinal Impact on Family Formation and Child Well-Being." Neuropsychopharmacology vol. 42(12), 12 Apr. 2017, pp. 2301-2313, ncbi.nlm.nih.gov/pmc/articles/PMC5645748/.

Chapter Six

76   *Recent research conducted by:* Abraham, Eyal, Ruth Feldman. "Oxytocin and Fathering." Fatherhood Global, 4 Jan. 2017, fatherhood.global/oxytocin-fathering/.

77   *According to Shelley E. Taylor:* Taylor, Shelley E. "Tend and Befriend Theory." Handbook of Theories of Social Psychology vol. 1, SAGE Publications Ltd, London, pp. 32-49, sk.sagepub.com/reference/hdbk_socialpsychtheories1/n3.xml.

79   *Like Dr. Taylor told:* DeAngelis, Tori. "The two faces of oxytocin." Monitor on Psychology vol 39(2), Feb. 2008, pp. 30. apa.org/monitor/feb08/oxytocin.

83   *In 2017, Cheryl:* Bort, Julie. "The 43 most powerful female engineers of 2017." Business Insider, 22 Feb. 2017, businessinsider.com/most-powerful-female-engineers-of-2017-2017-2.

Chapter Seven

91   *The World Economic Forum's:* "The Future of Jobs 2018." World Economic Forum, reports.weforum.org/future-of-jobs-2018/?doing_wp_cron=159 3454168.1190609931945800781250.

92   *Also, work is:* Cross, Rob, et al. "Collaborative Overload." Harvard Business Review, Jan-Feb. 2016. hbr.org/2016/01/collaborative-overload

92   *This is because:* Nowak, Martin A, Roger Highfield. SuperCooperators: Altruism, Evolution, and Why We Need Each Other to Succeed. Free Press, 2012.

93   *Armed with this:* Duhigg, Charles. "What Google Learned From Its Quest to Build the Perfect Team." The New York Times, 25 Feb. 2016, nytimes.com/2016/02/28/magazine/what-google-learned-from-its-quest-to-build-the-perfect-team.html.

93   *That conclusion led:* Edmondson, Amy. "Psychological Safety and Learning Behavior in Work Teams." Administrative Science Quarterly, vol. 44, no. 2, Jun. 1999, pp. 350–383, journals.sagepub.com/doi/abs/10.2307/2666999#articleCitationDownloadContainer.

94   *Other research conducted:* Goleman, Daniel. "What Makes a Leader?" Harvard Business Review, Jan. 2004, hbr.org/2004/01/what-makes-a-leader.

94   *When it comes to teams:* O'Neill, Thomas A., Eduardo Salas, "Creating high performance teamwork in organizations." Human Resource Management Review, vol. 28(4), Dec. 2018, pp.325-33. sciencedirect.com/science/article/abs/pii/S1053482217300736

Chapter Eight

101   *Up until now:* Blair-Loy, Mary, Stacy J. Williams. "The Male Model of the Career." Sociology of Work: An Encyclopedia, Thousand Oaks, CA: Sage Publications, 2013, us.sagepub.com/en-us/nam/sociology-of-work/book237017.

105   *Other studies have found:* Heilman, M. E., & Chen, J. J. (2005). Same behavior, different consequences: reactions to men's and women's altruistic citizenship behavior. Journal of Applied Psychology, 90(3), 431-441. Available at uccs.edu/Documents/dcarpent/altruism.pdf

108   This peer-based program: Mihalich-Levin, Lori. "Innovating the attorney-parent experience." Legal Evolution, 7 Jun. 2020, legalevolution.org/2020/06/innovating-the-attorney-parent-experience-166/

111   *Significant research indicates:* Erdmann-Sullivan, Heidi, "The Most Compelling Work-Life Stats of 2017 (so far)," Care@Work, 6 Oct. 2017, workplace.care.com/the-most-compelling-work-life-stats-of-2017-so-far.

103   *A landmark 2010 study:* Kelly, Erin L., et al. "Changing Workplaces to Reduce Work-Family Conflict: Schedule Control in a White-Collar Organization." American Sociological Association, vol. 76(2), 17 Mar. 2011, journals.sagepub.com/doiabs/10.1177/0003122411400056?journalCode=asra

Chapter Nine

125   *Evolutionary Anthropologist Richard Lee:* Lee, Richard B. "Hunter-Gatherers and Human Evolution: New Light on Old Debates." Annual Review of Anthropology vol. 47, 3 Aug. 2018, pp. 513-531, annualreviews.org/doi/abs/10.1146/annurev-anthro-102116-041448.

127   *As best-selling author:* Harari, Yuval Noah. "Why Technology Favors Tyranny." The Atlantic, Oct. 2018. theatlantic.com/magazine/archive/2018/10/yuval-noah-harari-technology-tyranny/568330/

Chapter Ten

129   *2010 Swedish study found:* Johansson, Elly-Ann, Swedish Institute of Labour Market Policy, "The effect of own and spousal parental leave on earnings", econstor.eu/bitstream/10419/45782/1/623752174.pdf

129   *And according to research;* Coltrane, Scott. Family Man: Fatherhood, Housework, and Gender Equity. Oxford University Press, 1997

129   *Researchers at Penn State;* "Parent–Child Shared Time From Middle Childhood to Late Adolescence: Developmental Course and Adjustment Female FoundersCorrelates": srcd.onlinelibrary.wiley.com/doi/abs/10.1111/j.1467-8624.2012.01826.x

130   *For Instance, one study:* Q3 2015 U.S. Employee Confidence Survey."
       Glassdoor. 2015. media.glassdoor.com/pr/press/pdf/ECS-Q32015-Supple-
       ment.pdf

133   *This test was a:* Blakeslee, Sandra. "What Other People Say May
       Change What You See." The New York Times, 28 Jun. 2005. nytimes.
       com/2005/06/28/science/what-other-people-say-may-change-what-you-see.
       html

133   *Gregory Berns, a professor:* Berns, Gregory S., et al. "Neurobiological Cor-
       relates of Social Conformity and Independence During Mental Rotation."
       Biological Psychiatry vol. 58(3), 1 Aug. 2005, pp. 245-253, pubmed.ncbi.
       nlm.nih.gov/15978553/.

134   *In the 1960's:* Schulte, Brigid. Overwhelmed: How to Work, Love, and
       Play When No One Has the Time. Picador Farrar, Straus and Giroux, 2015.

134   *In Sweden, for example:* Collins, Caitlyn, Making Motherhood Work: How
       Women Manage Careers and Caregiving, Princeton, Princeton University
       Press, 2019.

136   *Recent survey data indicates:* Edlund, Jonas. ISSP 2012 - Family, Work
       and Gender Roles IV.Umeå University, Department of Sociology, Swedish
       National Data Service, Version 3.0, 2015, doi.org/10.5878/002823

136   *In fact, all women:* Noland, Marcus, et al. "Is Gender Diversity Profitable?
       Evidence from a Global Survey." Peterson Institute for International Eco-
       nomics, Feb. 2016, piie.com/publications/wp/wp16-3.pdf

138   *In an Op-Ed:* Ohanian, Alexis. "Alexis Ohanian: Paternity Leave Was Cru-
       cial After the Birth of My Child, and Every Father Deserves It." The New
       York Times, The New York Times, 16 Apr. 2020, nytimes.com/2020/04/15/
       parenting/alexis-ohanian-paternity-leave.html.

       Chapter Eleven

143   *In 2018, Female founders:* Hinchliffe, Emma. "Funding For Female Found-
       ers Stalled at 2.2% of VC Dollars in 2018." Fortune, 28 Jan. 2019. fortune.
       com/2019/01/28/funding-female-founders-2018

148   *Mary Beth Ferrante, a member:* "27 Female 'FamTech' Founders Come
       Together To Care For Families During The COVID-19 Crisis" forbes.com/
       sites/marybethferrante/2020/03/17/27-female-famtech-founders-come-
       together-to-care-for-families-during-the-covid-19-crisis/?sh=1d3c765dd158

Conclusion

154   *In September alone, 865,000:* "Four Times More Women Than Men Dropped Out of the Labor Force in September" nwlc.org/resources/four-times-more-women-than-men-dropped-out-of-the-labor-force-in-september/

155   *Other recent reports:* Grundy, Kevin. "Insight: Virtual Back To School - Fewer Backpacks & More Laptops." Javatar.bluematrix.com/, JefData, 2020, javatar.bluematrix.com/.

155   *Pierre Omidyar's Hope Lab:* hopelab.org/

Amy Henderson is one of the nation's leading voices on the critical role parenting and caregiving will play in the future of work. Amy is the founding CEO of Tend-Lab, where she has been working with companies and their parents' groups at places like Salesforce, Accenture, Cloudflare, Airbnb, and Lululemon to optimize the workplace for parents. Amy also started and co-leads the Fam Tech Founders Collaborative, a network of over 130 founders who are solving for the needs of caregivers. Amy and her team at TendLab are working to change the game for working parents. Amy Henderson lives with her three children in the San Francisco Bay Area. *Tending* is her first book.

For more information, online events and to join the movement, visit AmyHenderson.org

 **NationBuilder**

NationBuilder envisions a world in which everyone has the freedom and opportunity to create what they are meant to create. Our mission is to build the infrastructure for a world of creators by helping leaders develop and organize thriving communities. Learn more about the software, stories, and community we offer to leaders at nationbuilder.com